Renée Mill has been working with people since 1973, first as an occupational therapist and then as a clinical psychologist. Over the years she has counselled hundreds of families and individuals with a range of problems. Listening intently to each individual's story, Renée realized that the way modern parents think is what immobilizes them from changing.

Renée has written articles for *Sydney Child / Melbourne Child / Canberra Child* that challenge current beliefs and have met with acclaim. She is regularly called on to talk at schools, community groups and even corporations about parenting beliefs and how they impact on one's energy levels.

Renée continues to work full time in her own private practice in Sydney with her team of associates to deliver effective counselling to parents and children. She also runs three weekly groups for mothers, women and parents.

Feedback from Renée Mill's parenting course,

Becoming a Better Parent

*Further information and Renée's NEW online
parenting course are available on her website:*

www.parentchildself.com.au

"Very helpful educational tools that help promote self-esteem" — Oded

"So much good information in the course, after listening to the CDs I would increase my evaluation to 20 out of 10. Taught us how to build the foundation of a warm, loving, organized home. One of the key factors was Renée as the teacher, her experience and knowing her" — Angus

"Really useful strategies to grow closer as family through values. I learnt how to communicate better, role model and some behavioral techniques" — Yakir

"Lots of excellent practical information, it made us evaluate and discuss things as a couple that we hadn't before. We learnt different methods of getting the children to comply rather than using punishment" — Rachel

"Outstanding tools and framework to model whole home environment and relationship with your child. Practical, logical and 'implementable' and focused on the positive. Made me consciously aware of the positive way of parenting. I learnt how to impart my value system to my child in everything I do and how to think through my own issues or state of mind before interacting with my child" — Tania

"I found the course very helpful and achievable. The course taught me how to work with the child from scratch, dealing with our own issues and treating it all with a wholistic approach" — Paula

"The course was practical, backed up with professional knowledge. Since the course I have thought about my response to behaviors and my relationship with my partner" — Vanessa

"We feel like we have been helped in literally avoiding hitting the brick wall into which we were careening — thank you. Our self-esteem was built-up, we have become more organized and learnt to work as a team with enlightened methods of behavioral intervention" — Haylene

No Sweat Parenting

Six Parenting Myths Debunked!

Renée Mill

BSc (OT) BA Hons MA (Clin Psych) MAPS

Renée Mill
and Associates

Renée Mill Clinical Psychologist Pty Ltd
www.parentchildself.com.au

ISBN 978-0-9805859-0-2
First published 2009
Text © Renée Mill 2009

Cover, illustrations and design by
David Andor / Wave Source Design
www.wavesource.com.au

A Cataloguing-in-Publication entry for this work can be
found in the National Library of Australia.

Table of Contents

Parents today are tired, overwhelmed and stretched for time.

Most of the parents I work with are genuinely loving and committed to doing the best for their children. They normally consult with me because they worry that they are not doing their best. Helen is an example of a mother who worries about her parenting:

> *Helen came to my rooms accompanied by her husband. They told me that they have no real problems with their two children Zak and Zara. However, they are concerned that they are not enriching the lives of their youngsters enough and wanted guidelines on how to fill their children's days.*

Alternatively parents consult with me when they are experiencing difficulties with a child's behavior. Joe is one such parent:

Joe walked into my consulting rooms complaining that his daughter Emily does not listen to him when he asks her to do something like brush her teeth. He believes that he has tried everything but nothing has worked so far. Occasionally he gets so angry that he explodes but afterwards he regrets it. He asks me for some strategies to fix the problem.

Twenty years ago I would have jumped right in with suggestions of how to enrich the world of Zak and Zara and strategies for getting Emily to comply.

> Over time, however, I noticed that the suggestions were often not implemented and that the parents' frustrations remained. I decided to analyse why there is a gap between good advice and implementation.

By listening carefully to hundreds of parents over many years, I noticed that universal beliefs have sprung up that color the parenting of modern parents. It suddenly hit me that frequently my client and I were not on the same page when it came to our philosophies about parenting. This would account for the gap.

For example, Helen (in the example above) did not need suggestions of how to enrich her children's lives. They were already busy, engaged with multiple activities in their hectic lifestyle. Helen was really looking for reassurance that she is an excellent mother. Because my suggestions would have been about cutting down, slowing down and emphasizing quality over quantity, Helen would not have heeded my advice.

In the other example given, Joe needed to learn how to be assertive with his daughter. However, as long as he worries that being firm may be damaging, he will not implement my tried and tested remedies.

> More and more I have seen the power of beliefs in determining parenting strategies and I have come to understand and accept that meaningful improvement can only occur once helpful beliefs are in place.

Now that I am wiser, I do not jump in with practical strategies but take time to explore the beliefs held by the parents. This exploration is an important part of establishing treatment goals.

With Helen, I explored what 'enriched' meant for her and what she wanted to achieve with her children. Once I understood her perspective, I encouraged her to question whether or not being busy and participating in multiple activities was achieving her goals.

Helen stayed stuck in her thought system and I knew then that it was futile to suggest alternatives. I respected her choice and left her with some new ideas to ponder.

In Joe's case, we spoke a lot about the difference between being aggressive and being assertive. We also teased out differences between authoritarian and authoritative. Joe soaked up the information I provided about self-esteem and how it is best developed. Once he was clear about the concepts, he gladly implemented some strategies that required him to be firm.

> This book is written as a response to the needs of parents and, I believe, the needs of children.

Parents and children are struggling under the weight of erroneous and unhelpful beliefs. This book is not about changing the behavior of your child outside of a context. It is about realizing that your behavior and that of your child occurs as a response to a belief system.

By providing you with alternative, helpful beliefs I hope to empower you to change the space within which you operate. This in turn will create an environment that is conducive to personal fulfilment and growth for everybody.

Chapter One

The Power of Beliefs

Beliefs are a guiding force in your behaviors and life choices.

What you believe is responsible for how you feel and behave. Sometimes you might think that you are behaving randomly but, in truth, your belief system has motivated your behavior. will explain what I mean with the EBB FLOW model.

EBB FLOW Model
E = Event
B = Belief about the event
B = Behavior
F = Feelings
L = Language
O = Outcome
W = Win/Win

E = Event

This can be any event that happens in your life. It is any occurrence, no matter how small, that takes place in your day-to-day activities. In the illustration at the beginning of this chapter, the event is that a toddler is running around wildly. Imagine this is your toddler.

B = Belief

When you see your toddler running around, you will automatically have a belief about his behavior. You may not be aware of the belief since it races through your mind automatically, unconsciously and very, very quickly.

The belief can be positive or negative. For instance, if you are thinking that it is great that your toddler has the opportunity to run around and get some exercise, the belief is positive. Alternatively, if you are thinking that it is embarrassing that he runs around so wildly, the belief is negative.

B = Behavior

Your behavior during an event will be determined by your belief. If you have the positive belief that it is great that he is running around, you will act in a kind and accepting manner toward your child. However, if you have the negative belief, namely, that his behavior is embarrassing, you will act in a critical and angry manner.

F = Feelings

Your automatic belief will influence the way you feel as well. The positive belief will result in you feeling happy for your child while the negative belief will result in you feeling embarrassed at his wild behavior.

L = Language

How you speak, the tone and words you use, are directly related to your belief about an event. If your belief is the positive one and you truly are happy that your child is having exercise, you will speak lovingly and use terms of endearment. Conversely, if your belief is negative, your tone toward your child could be aggressive and your words harsh.

O = Outcome

The outcome of an event is totally connected to your initial belief about it. The positive belief will ensure a positive outcome, with your child enjoying his run and you feeling calm and loving. The negative belief will assuredly result in both you and your child feeling bad.

W = Win/Win

The purpose of this book is to help you to achieve a winning solution as a parent. You want to be calm and loving as much as possible, with a happy and loved child at the receiving end of your affection.

The expression "ebb and flow" is a very optimistic one when it refers to human behavior. It implies that your behavior is flexible and can easily and quickly change by merely changing your thoughts.

Once you learn how to move from one thought to another, you will find it easy to behave like the parent you want to be.

Practical examples of the EBB FLOW model

The basic philosophy of the EBB FLOW model is that life's events are neutral in and of themselves. No event is intrinsically good or bad. (I am not talking about behaviors here. Behaviors can be good or bad but events are neutral). What makes us react in a positive or negative manner to an event is the belief we ascribe to it.

> ### Example
>
> Event: it is raining = neutral
>
> Belief: rain = flood = damage = negative emotions
>
> Belief: rain = nourishing = good to relieve the drought = happy emotions

Let me now illustrate the point that every event is neutral but can be met with two totally different responses:

> *When Mary came home after shopping and found that her daughter had left a trail of cereal on the floor, she said nothing. She hugged her daughter and cleaned up after her. Josey on the other hand got very angry when her daughter left the same amount of mess.*

Since mess in and of itself is neutral, the different responses of Mary and Josey can be ascribed to the different beliefs they each carry about mess. Mary believes that mess made by a three year old is to be expected and she accepts that it is her role as a mother to clean up after her child until she is old enough to do it for herself. Josey, however, finds mess unacceptable and resents having to clean up after anyone. Mary is telling herself, "this is normal", while Josey is telling herself, "I cannot stand this. It should not be happening".

Another example involves two fathers putting their four year old sons to sleep at night:

Peter and Jack both work hard all day and come home tired. Peter loves putting his son to sleep and is grateful that he has the opportunity to spend some time in the day with him. Jack feels obligated to put his son to sleep and resents it. Jack believes that he should have down time at the end of the day and putting his son to sleep deprives him of this time.

Putting a child to bed is neutral. What you tell yourself about it will determine your emotions and your behavior.

As you can see, beliefs have a powerful effect on us. They are the source of much of your parental unhappiness.

Beliefs are also the source of much frustration and fatigue. Changing beliefs will be the springboard for changing the patterns of behavior that now lead to exhaustion.

The purpose of this book is to assist you:
- to feel less alone in your struggles as a parent,
- to identify the beliefs you carry around in your head,
- to provide alternative, realistic beliefs that will improve your feelings about parenting,

- to improve the quality of your parenting,
- to learn tools that will help you change your behavior,
- to enjoy your children,

How empowering is that? You do not need to change your life around, or be a different person to be a happy and effective parent. All you need to do is take on practical, realistic and helpful beliefs.

Change *is* possible.

Perhaps you are sceptical that you can change. You may have tried to change in the past but over time resorted to the same negative behaviors. The truth is that it is possible to change, but for that to happen, repetition is necessary.

To replace old beliefs with new ones, you need to keep challenging the old beliefs and verbalizing the new ones. Just saying a belief once will not make a lasting change.

Exercise

Whenever an old belief pops into your head, say to yourself: "STOP. This is not true. XXXX is true". Say it aloud, if possible.

Practical Example

You walk into the living room and your son has left some toys on the floor. You think to yourself, "This child does not respect my wishes. If he did he would clean up after himself as I always tell him to do." You find yourself getting angry. As you self-monitor and realize what you are thinking and feeling, say aloud, "STOP! This is not necessarily true. The truth is that my son left a mess because he is four years old and needs reminding. He is not as focused on mess as I am. He moved onto his next activity and forgot about it. It has nothing to do with lack of respect for me. He is just being a four -year- old. Let me think of a way to help him to remember in the future."

Beliefs are not difficult to change. They will change with repetition. However, emotions are extremely difficult to control once you are in the grip of one. For example, if you are angry with your child and start to yell, you will find it difficult to stop. However, if you work on your belief system and re-frame the way you view your child/mess/perfection etc., then it acts preventively and you will not become angry to start with.

By working on beliefs, which are the second step of the EBB FLOW model, you will be able to feel and behave in ways that result in the win/win outcome you desire.

Myths and age-old truths

The beliefs that you carry around have been formed by many different sources, such as the values your parents instilled in you, societal and cultural influences and your own experience over time. It is not my aim to explain where beliefs come from. Nor is it my aim to attack any particular value system. However, it is my intention to point out common beliefs that put added pressure on modern parents and are not necessarily helpful in your quest as a parent. It is also my goal to empower you with replacement beliefs that I passionately believe are helpful to both you and your child.

Conclusion

Our behavior, feelings and language are all influenced by our beliefs. You may not even be aware of the beliefs that you have absorbed from the world around you. When you feel unhappy or angry or stressed, examine what you are telling yourself. You will be amazed to find that by simply changing what you are telling yourself at that moment, you will change your whole experience and behavior.

When I think right, I am a relaxed and loving parent. Therefore, "Think right, feel good".

Try this:

Think for yourself. Just because something is fashionable it does not mean that it is true or beneficial. Trust your own instincts and experience. Challenge the latest ideas being put out by society and investigate them thoroughly before you take them on.

If I am late for his first swimming lesson, I will never forgive myself!

myth 1

"I must be a perfect parent"

A perfect parent is an oxymoron.

Human beings are fallible, mortal and vulnerable. Yet we live in an age when marketing experts try and convince us otherwise. Consumers are told that it is possible to look young indefinitely if the right face cream is bought and that if you read the tips in a particular magazine, a perfect marriage is attainable.

The underlying message being "sold" is:
- Perfection is possible if you get the right advice,
- Perfection is possible in a very short space of time,
- Perfection is possible with very little effort,
- If you have not achieved your goal, it is because you have done something wrong.

Every one of these messages creates stress and leads to fatigue once they become beliefs. These beliefs can be parent-specific.

Unrealistic beliefs

- Being a perfect parent is possible if you get the right advice/ take your child to the best therapist/ read the latest parenting guide/listen to the guru of the month.
- Having a perfect relationship with your child is possible in a short space of time.
- With just a few tips you can achieve whatever your heart desires.
- Helping your child develop into the perfect child can happen quickly and with little effort.
- When the desired result is taking time, or requires hard work, it must be because you have made wrong choices or are not a good person or are a failure.

Sometimes these beliefs are articulated differently. Here is a list of comments parents have made to me over the years that indicate they subscribe to the perfection belief.

- I must be patient all the time.
- I should be available 24/7.
- I must give the correct response every time my child is upset.
- I try never to be angry.
- I cannot forgive myself if I shout.
- My child deserves my attendance at every soccer training session.
- I make sure that I am available to do homework every afternoon.

- I prefer to take my child places rather than car pool.

Questions can also reveal the "perfection" belief:

- Will I damage my child if the babysitter puts him to bed once a week?
- How harmful is it if I shout when my child does not listen?
- Is it OK to go out with our friends on a Saturday night?
- Sometimes I am a little late collecting my daughter from kindy and she has to sit with the teacher. Am I a terrible dad?
- I want to exercise but I worry my son will resent it one day. What are the statistics on that?

Here is an example of how this "perfection myth" plays out in family life:

Tessa is a loving mom who works in the mornings and is able to spend every afternoon with her children. She wants to be there for them and to show her offspring that she is devoted to them. This year she placed her three- year- old daughter in pre-school, which ends at 3pm. Her son, who is in year one, finishes school at 3pm too, and it is physically impossible for Tessa to collect him. She has arranged a car pool with a friendly neighbor and, by 3:30pm, she and her son are reunited. Nonetheless, every day she worries that she has let her son down.

Here is another example:

> *Fred grew up in a family where verbal communication was rare. They were loving and physically affectionate but not good with words. As an adult, Fred has found it hard to express himself verbally but when he reads an article on parenting that stresses the importance of choosing the right words, he feels like a failure.*
>
> *When his son is upset, Fred cuddles him and reassures him, and his son appears to be very content. However, Fred worries that he is not doing enough and wishes he had some clever phrases he could throw out at the "right" moment.*

In both of the above examples, the children concerned are happy, well-adjusted children. Their parents' "omissions" are not harmful or serious at all. The needs of the children are clearly being met in an adequate way. It is only Tessa's unrealistic desire to be available to her offspring 24/7 that is causing her distress. Similarly, it is only Fred's insecure thought that there is a better way of doing things (for which he is ill-equipped) that is stressing him out.

The parenting relationship involves two imperfect human beings.

Every parent I know is unprepared for the individuality and determination of their child which manifests from day one. This is a major contributing factor to difficulties faced by parents.

Margaret's situation illustrates this point beautifully:

Margaret always wanted to breastfeed. She had dreams of idyllic days rocking in her armchair, nursing her baby. When she had her son Nigel, she tried to make her dream a reality but, guess what? Nigel did not want to suck. He is what you call a "lazy feeder". Sucking a nipple requires effort, and after a few attempts, little Nigel would pucker his lips and refuse to open them. In desperation, Margaret gave him the bottle, from which he happily drank. Nigel, at three days old, was making his mark.

Max's daughter proved to be his teacher:

Max is a very affectionate person. He was overjoyed when he had a daughter and looked forward to a warm and cuddly relationship. He did not know that some children do not like to be cuddled. His daughter Tammy did not enjoy being tickled, hugged or kissed. As she got older, she ran away from it more and more. Max had to learn to let the physical contact be on her terms.

Both Nigel and Tammy had their needs met by their parents. They each had their own "needs level" and did not enjoy what their parents wanted to "inflict" on them. Being a good parent is mostly about giving children what they need rather than trying to fit some theoretical mould.

Margaret could feel satisfied that she had met Nigel's need by bottle-feeding, which means that she behaved as a caring parent. Max, while feeling disappointed at the lack of reciprocity in showing affection, could still feel reassured that his daughter's needs in that area were being met.

Life is full of unexpected surprises

Life is another major impediment to achieving perfection. Every adult has experienced the frustration of not reaching a well-planned goal because life interfered.

Mary is an earth-mother type and could not wait until she had her first child. She ate healthily and did yoga during her pregnancy and eagerly looked forward to a natural birth. This was not to be. Six weeks before her due date she went into early labor as the baby was in distress. Her little girl, Samantha, was born by Caesarean section. This was necessary to save her life. She had a severe breathing difficulty and could not be breastfed or held for several weeks. Mary's plans for bonding with her baby were shattered and it took a long while for her to feel connected. Mary's intentions were wonderful but life had other plans.

Jeremy had a difficult upbringing. He had been sent away to boarding school and he hated it. He promised himself that he would be an involved father giving his children a warm home and lots of love. When his first child turned two, he lost his job.

After several months of looking, he found a job three hours away. Jeremy felt that, in order to provide for his family, he had no choice but to move there and come home on weekends. He had desperately wanted to live up to his promise but his life's circumstances pushed him in a different direction.

Since breaking your back to be perfect is unachievable and exhausting, it is much healthier to be realistic.

You will experience less stress when you see yourself for who you are rather than trying to become supermom or superdad.

The secondary gain of striving for perfection

Striving to be perfect is a way of convincing yourself and your family that you really do love them; not striving might seem like copping out. For example, in Mary's case, she worried that if she stopped feeling bad about not having a perfect beginning, her daughter would think she did not care about her. In a similar vein, Jeremy was concerned that if he stopped apologizing, his children would think that he was living his dream and did not care about their everyday life.

This is the message they were giving their children:

1. **Life can be perfect**
2. **I can be perfect**
3. **I owe you**
4. **The world owes you**

When you give this message, it not only adds a lot of stress but can perpetuate this belief for future generations. Rather than spending your life beating yourself up for not being the perfect parent, accept that life is not perfect and you are not perfect and discover that you can live very happily in spite of this. Or, perhaps you can live very happily *because* of the imperfections.

Realistic beliefs

There are several realistic beliefs that will assist you to be more relaxed about your parenting abilities:

- Life presents many obstacles,
- Parenting presents many obstacles,
- I am a human being. I can only do the best I can with the tools that I have at the time,
- I make mistakes on occasion. This teaches my child to cope with other people's imperfections,
- When I am relaxed about being imperfect, I am teaching my child that it is normal to make mistakes,
- By educating my child that life and people are not perfect, I am preparing him for a happier life.

These beliefs are explained below and will help you to feel better about your fallibility. Say them even if you do not believe them, and they will eventually become part of your way of thinking.

Life presents many obstacles

Life is full of struggles, and relationship issues, and demands. Not everyone can achieve the Hollywood family image of the white picket fence, two dogs, two cars and two children (one boy and one girl, of course) and a lovely home in a leafy avenue close to dad's work. When your world is not working out in the way you had hoped, you will increase your stress levels when you tell yourself, "This should not be happening. Life is meant to be different," or "I am the only person who has it so hard". Alternatively, you can lower stress by acknowledging that life is full of struggles for everyone so you might as well get on with solving the problems without too much resentment.

> Let us restate the belief in terms of parenting: **parenting presents many obstacles.**

In other words, it is realistic to accept that no parent can give their child a perfect existence. Sometimes you will make a bad decision such as allowing your child to stay up too late. At other times you may behave badly because you are in a bad mood.

Sometimes your child will have a tantrum and not listen to you. Often your personality and that of your child will clash. Sometimes, no matter how hard you try, your marriage will fail and you will not be around much for your child. There may be times when you are grieving the loss of a loved one and you are emotionally removed from your child for a while. A handicap may prevent you from running with your child or hugging her.

You may have wanted to provide your child with material possessions but your financial means prevented it. You may have desperately wanted to be a stay-at-home mother but your husband leaving you has forced you to work full time. You want to help your child with his maths but you have no clue about maths.

The list of possible life events that interfere with being a perfect parent is endless.

"I am a human being. I can only do the best I can with the tools I have at the moment".

I am a human being. I am not all-powerful and therefore cannot provide my child with every possible thing. Nor can I be everywhere at once. As a result, there are times my child will have to wait. I can only do the best I can with the tools I have at any given time. Tools include, my personality, emotional state, financial means, time constraints, family support, living conditions and other life circumstances.

> *"I make mistakes on occasions which teaches my child to cope with other people's imperfections".*

I make mistakes on occasion and that is not the end of the world. In fact, it is good for my child to learn to cope with other people's idiosyncrasies.

As an adult, he will have to work with people who are not perfect. As a spouse he will have to learn to tolerate his partner's differences. It teaches my child to have realistic expectations of the people in his life.

> *"When I am relaxed about being imperfect, I am teaching my child it is normal to make mistakes".*

When I am relaxed about being imperfect, I am breaking the cycle of the need for perfection that our society has set up. I am teaching my child that it is normal to make mistakes. I am demonstrating to my child that she is normal as she, too, makes mistakes.

> *"By educating my child that life and people are not perfect, I am preparing him for a happier life".*

When my child has internalized the realistic view that neither life nor people are perfect, he will not feel deprived when things do not go his way. He will be able to tolerate frustration, an important life skill. He will be more able to enjoy his life for what it is rather than wishing it was different / better / perfect.

Affirmations

Changing your beliefs to more realistic beliefs will make your life so much simpler. It will remove many of the pressures of trying to be perfect. Below are some affirmations that will assist you to feel good about your parenting skills.

You can feel good about your parenting even if you are not perfect. When you can endorse yourself for a job well done, you will feel competent as a parent in a realistic way.

Affirmation 1:

"I endorse myself for doing the best I can with the tools I have at the moment".

It is vitally important to learn how to endorse yourself for a job well done. Endorsing yourself means acknowledging that you are doing OK. When you work at a job, you get a pay check, which validates your effort. You may even get a compliment from your manager. However, as a parent you get no recognition from others and you are bombarded with information of how to do things "right" or better. Therefore, you need to learn the art of recognizing your own efforts.

What is extremely helpful is to learn to endorse yourself for doing the best you can with the tools you have. What tools do I mean? I mean your personality for one. If you have a short fuse and you work on staying calm, you can endorse yourself for trying your best to calm yourself (as opposed to whipping yourself because you have a short fuse). Conversely, if you are a cold fish and struggle to be affectionate with your kids, endorse yourself for struggling to improve rather than focusing on how cold you are.

Endorsing yourself for effort is in no way an opportunity to excuse bad behavior. Being angry the majority of the time is not acceptable, and you need to work on managing your anger. You may even have to get professional help. However, along the way, you can keep endorsing yourself for doing the best you can despite your shortcomings. This is more motivating than focusing on how terrible you are, especially since it is not your preference to be this way.

Another tool is your life circumstances. If you have limited resources, you will be limited in what you can offer. The question is whether you are doing the best you can with your limited resources. If the answer is yes, then go ahead and endorse yourself for doing so.

For example, if you have little money but you manage to pay for your child to have violin tuition, endorse yourself for that instead of feeling inadequate because you were not able to send your child to a private school. If you are a single parent, endorse yourself for the time you are able to give your child rather than beating yourself up for not being a stay-at-home mom.

Affirmation 2:

"I endorse myself for effort and not for success."

With this tool, you look at success in life and parenting in terms of what is in your control (your effort) rather than outcome. This way you can feel adequate even if the results are not always what you had hoped for.

In the earlier examples, Margaret had wanted to breast-feed but Nigel preferred the bottle. Margaret can focus on the fact that her plan failed and therefore feel she is a failure as a mother or she can endorse herself for trying her best to provide breast milk for her son.

She can feel gratified that she has done her best although "success" was not the outcome.

Max wanted so much to be a physically affectionate dad. He did his best to encourage that scenario as he believed it was a good direction to take. Tammy, his daughter, did not want that level of touch. However, that in no way detracts from Max's efforts and good intentions.

Max can endorse himself for the continuing effort he puts in to meet Tammy's needs according to her comfort zone.

Jeremy can feel terrible about having to work away from home. Alternatively, he can endorse himself for supporting his family financially and for being the best father he can in the situation in which he finds himself. He is Jeremy. He is not anyone else. Well done, Jeremy, for prioritizing the effort to be a loving father in very difficult circumstances.

Affirmation 3:

"I do not make excuses for bad behavior."

When poor behavior is chronic, you need to take action as soon as possible.

Let us say that you have a short fuse. You are working hard on staying calm. You can endorse yourself for effort and feel good at the effort you are making. However, if you keep saying, "This is how I am/ I cannot help it/ it is because of my star sign/ it is a function of my stress etc," then you clearly do not believe you can be better.

We are looking for middle ground here. I am encouraging you to give up the unrealistic demand for perfection. I am saying it is impossible to never lose your temper. Do not walk around feeling like a criminal because you were angry once last week. Humans make mistakes. I am *not* saying that it is OK to continually "make mistakes" that cause your children to suffer.

Chronic anger needs to be corrected. However, every little victory you make should be endorsed by you and seen realistically as a step closer to better behavior overall. You are not aiming for perfect behavior but for better behavior.

In the same vein, if you are away a lot of the time, you need to strive to be around for your child as much as is humanly possible when you are at home. You cannot excuse yourself by saying, "This is just how it is. Tough". You can say, "This is the way my life is right now. Life is not perfect. However, despite the difficulties, I endorse myself for trying my best to be around emotionally for my children when I am home and by maintaining phone contact".

Whilst you have learned to accept reality, and you realize that you do not need to hate yourself and your life when things do not go smoothly, you can still strive to realistically improve things. Within the constraints, are you doing the best you can? If the answer is yes, then you are on the way to being a happy and adequate parent.

Conclusion

There is no such thing as a perfect parent. It is much more helpful to accept yourself; correct bad behavior where necessary and endorse yourself for the good things that you do achieve. Living with imperfections and enjoying life will also teach your child to do the same.

A real relationship with my child means both of us being human and imperfect!

Try this:

This week, admit to your child that you do not know something. Feel good about being human and free from the pressure of knowing it all.

If you would like a chart of these affirmations to hang up as a daily reminder, please go to my website **www.parentchildself.com** *and download.*

myth 2

"If I am firm, my child will have low self-esteem"

Building self-esteem is a great goal.

"Self-esteem" has become a buzzword equated with good parenting. No doubt, you have felt the extreme pressure of society to focus on building the self-esteem of your child. In truth, it is an important goal because a healthy self-esteem will have a positive impact on your child's ability to be successful at work and in relationships.

Over the past twenty-five years, at the same time that self-esteem was recognized as vital for good mental health, abuse was recognized as detrimental for mental health. Suddenly terms like physical abuse, mental abuse and sexual abuse became common expressions. Educators and state authorities have thankfully done a lot to protect children from these atrocities. Whereas previously abuse was a tightly kept secret, today terrible things are perpetrated against children pretty much out in the open.

You are probably starting to see how parallel knowledge about these issues has contributed to a kind of cross-over:

if building self-esteem is good and being abusive is bad, then a good way of building self-esteem must be to bend over backwards to be nice.

The huge gap between bending over backwards to please, on one hand, and being abusive and harmful on the other, has been overlooked by many parents today who tend to adopt the extreme view of being nice at all costs.

Being accommodating when it is inappropriate isn't helpful to your child.

Who is the boss?

It is not uncommon to find families today in which a two-year-old infant is running the show because his parents want him to feel good about himself.

Jared is a good example of this phenomenon.

Last week a grandfather called me as he felt that he was going to explode. His daughter, who lives overseas, was visiting for three weeks with her two-year-old son, Jared. The grandfather reported that from 5 pm every afternoon, his daughter would start negotiating with Jared about having a bath. The negotiation went something like this:

5pm: *"Jared darling, would you like to have a bath now?"*
        "NO."
        "Okay, darling."

5:30pm: *"Jared darling, would you like to have a bath now?"*
        "NO."

"Okay, darling."

6 pm: *"Jared, I think you really should have a bath now."*

"I don't want to."

"Why not, sweetheart?"

"Because."

"Okay, sweetheart, you tell me when you are ready to have a bath."

Sometimes Jared would actually agree to have a bath, to everyone's relief. Frequently, however, he would continue to refuse and then a tussle over going to bed would follow the tussle over having a bath. Sometimes Jared's mom would explode and force him to have a bath. However, most often she would be too exhausted to fight and would let him call the shots even if this meant he would go to bed dirty.

Jared's refusal to bathe means that he is not learning good life habits. Moreover, his refusal totally interferes with the routine of the entire household. Neither Jared's mom nor his grandparents can eat on time or plan an outing as they have no idea whether or not Jared will comply. In Jared's family, he is the boss.

I have no doubt that if I questioned Jared's mom, she would say that she is prioritizing Jared's self-esteem and therefore she does not want to push him around. She wants him to feel comfortable with the decisions being made. She also wants him to feel that he is important in the family. Jared's mom believes she is doing a good thing.

Maria provides another good example:

Maria is a four-year-old who still exhibits tantrums. When her father tries to discipline her, she throws a fit, frightening everyone around her. If she does not feel like going to bed, she will throw herself onto the floor and scream till her mother says to her father, "Let's not upset Maria. I will give her a hug and calm her down and later we will try to get her to sleep again".

Sometimes they have to cancel plans to be with friends because they are afraid to leave Maria at home with a baby-sitter when she is upset.

Maria's parents have no private time or space, but they think it may be worth it because they are doing everything in their power to keep Maria happy. Maria controls her parents through her tantrums.

Maria's parents believe that giving in to her tantrums will ensure her future happiness. They also believe that if they continue in this patient and giving manner, Maria's behavior will improve spontaneously. They do not realize that Maria will not learn appropriate behaviors through maturing or luck — she needs to be taught.

You might be feeling that I am exaggerating and that in your home the situation is not so severe. I am not exaggerating, I assure you. If you answer the following questions truthfully, you may see how often you allow your child to dominate.

- When you try to be firm with your child and he gets upset, do you tend to back down?
- Have you ever refused to buy your child a toy that he does not need and then gone back to the shop the next day to buy it as you worried overnight that you were too harsh?

- Do you remember a time when your child intruded into your private space with your partner and you allowed it as you were concerned that your child would feel rejected?
- How often have you set a consequence for your child and then let it go as you do not want him to suffer in any way?
- Have you given up insisting that your four-year-old sleep in his own bed because you worry that he may feel insecure?
- Do you allow your child to set the agenda for the day, even though you may be inconvenienced?

Engaging in any of the above behaviors allows your child to make important decisions. Bending over backwards to please puts him in charge in many ways.

The secondary gain of being soft

When you give in to your child's demands, your primary conscious motive is to build self-esteem. However, there is frequently a secondary, less conscious motive, which satisfies something in you: your need to be liked. Let's face it; we all want to be liked. It is very hard to tolerate disapproval, and whose approval is more important to us than that of our beloved child?

This is an anomaly of our generation. In previous generations, children sought their parents' approval, now it's the other way around! We want to feel liked. Actually, we want to be loved and affirmed. Moreover this yearning feeds into the belief, "I must be a perfect parent". Our thoughts go something like this: "If my child is happy with me, then I must be doing a good job. I like feeling adequate so let me keep trying to make my child happy by continuing to give in to his demands".

The age-old truth

The simple answer to 'Who is the boss?' is: 'You, the parent'. It was actually a rhetorical question. How could it possibly make sense to have a toddler in charge?

You may think you are doing your child a favor by giving him so much power, but that thinking is mistaken. Let us examine some of the erroneous beliefs that have pervaded our culture and resulted in children being given too much power.

Erroneous beliefs about building self-esteem

- Self-esteem is primarily built through being sweet and complimentary.
- Being firm will damage a child's self-esteem.
- Setting boundaries will make a child feel helpless.
- A child is capable of making decisions.
- A child can understand the implications of a decision.
- A child knows what is important in life.
- Parents are there to serve their child.
- A child likes to feel powerful and that is good for self-esteem.
- Building self-esteem is the most important part of being a good parent.
- All a child needs is good self-esteem in order to be happy and successful.

There is a little bit of truth in each of these beliefs. By fine tuning them to be more realistic, you will be able to reclaim your position as parent in a way that does not compromise your intense need to build your child's self-esteem.

Realistic beliefs

There are several realistic beliefs about self-esteem that will make your life much easier. Let's face it, having to be nice all the time can be gruelling. Also, being dominated by a two-year-old is not much fun.

Learning what truly enhances self-esteem will help you to cope much better but, most importantly, will achieve your goal of building your child's self-esteem.

- Being firm and harsh are two separate things.
- A child needs his parent to be firm in order to feel secure.
- Taking charge means being a caring captain of a ship.
- An adult has greater life experience, wisdom and conceptual ability than a child.
- There is more to self-esteem than feeling happy in the moment.

Being firm and harsh are two separate things.

Being harsh means doing something that causes pain to a child. For example, when a parent calls a child a name or pushes him around, that is harshness. Punishment that is excessively severe for a minor infraction is harsh. Teasing or humiliating, name-calling, setting unrealistic goals and/or demanding excellence all the time are harsh things to do.

Being firm, on the other hand, means setting a boundary so that your child knows exactly what is expected of him. It also means creating a lifestyle with consistency and routine so that your child knows what to expect every day.

It is good for a child's self-esteem when a parent is firm and yes, it is damaging to a child's self-esteem when a parent is harsh or abusive. They are two different things and there is a huge gap between them .

A child needs his parent to be firm in order to feel secure

Children often feel helpless, relying on their parents to be the intermediary between them and the huge, frightening world. If mom and dad are sure of themselves and make decisions that they stick by, their children will feel good about themselves.

Let us revisit the example about Jared and his mom.

If his mom is not convinced that a bath a day is necessary and if she is inconsistent about implementing bath routines, Jared will feel insecure. His only strategy then is to keep challenging his mom's authority in the hope that eventually she will prove her strength. Jared assuredly wonders to himself, "If I am stronger than mom, then who can I rely on to feel safe in this huge world of ours?"

Similarly, Maria, who was presented in the earlier example, feels out of control and desperate. She has developed a habit of throwing tantrums in order to force her parents to take charge, but it has backfired. She is like a kidnapper who has taken a hostage but, with time, realizes that she has nowhere to go. The kidnapper wishes someone would take charge and solve the situation even if it means some jail time.

Too much power with nowhere to go is frightening. Maria keeps acting in extreme ways, hoping that her parents will worry enough to do something to rescue her. She is calling out to her parents, "Hello, can you be the adult here and take charge?" but it is not working.

Unlike animals that only care for their young for a short time, humans care for their young for decades. Surely there is a message in that? Surely we are being instructed that children need to be parented, as they are incapable of coping in the wild, and will only be ready in twenty years or so.

Children need care, direction and safety, and the way that they feel secure is when the adult in their life takes charge.

You may be agreeing with me so far, but I know that you still have a niggling doubt: how can you take charge without being authoritarian? How can you be the boss yet still build your child's self-esteem?

Taking charge means being a caring captain of a ship

How would you feel if you were on a cruise with an ingratiating captain? He wants you to have a pleasurable cruise and therefore allows you to plan the route. You want to go to a desert island but you do not know that to get there you have to sail through treacherous waters. Instead of instructing you about the dangers, and planning a safe route, he agrees to your request. His need to please you results in a difficult and stormy journey that you do not enjoy at all. When you hit a storm, he sweetly asks you to go downstairs but you refuse and accuse him of being mean and spoiling your fun. He allows you to stay on deck, in the life-threatening gale force winds, and you are petrified. He ordered delicious food for the journey but you demand something else at meal times, forcing him to leave his post to arrange shipment of the new food.

At first you feel powerful, happy even. However, with time you start to feel worried. Are you ever going to get to your destination, you wonder? Will you get there safely? Does the captain really know what he is doing? After all, you have placed your life in his hands. Does he take his job seriously when he seems so easily distracted by trivialities?

I am sure you are getting the picture. You would feel really happy and secure in the long term if the captain set firm rules and guidelines and stuck by them. He can still be kind to you and treat you well but he knows how important his job is in getting you to your destination safely. His focus is on your well-being and if that means that you are angry when he sends you downstairs in a storm, so be it.

The analogy is obvious. You can be loving, kind and wonderful to your child, but he needs direction. He needs you to take charge when there is a problem. He needs you to teach him how the ship is best managed so that he will benefit overall. He needs a savvy captain and not a wimpy friend. In short, he wants and needs a wise adult in his life, one who can make him feel safe.

The good news is that by being a caring captain who takes charge, you will not harm your child in any way. On the contrary, you will be building his self-esteem immeasurably. A child who feels safe through living with direction, consistency and order flourishes emotionally.

An adult has greater life experience, wisdom and conceptual ability than a child

We know from child development research that small children are not able to conceptualize in the way that adults do. In simple terms, this means that a child cannot see the consequences of his actions. Moreover, a child has little life experience and cannot possibly understand the importance of things like personal hygiene.

He also has no idea about relationships and how they work. Nor does he understand the difference between good and bad choices in life. So, how ridiculous is it to allow a small child to make decisions about running a home?

A child does need to feel empowered and you do this by giving him choices like: which shirt would you like to wear today? But you do not give him a choice about wearing a jumper when it is below zero outside.

Your child is a child; he does not understand what "below zero" means. He does not see the consequences of going out into the cold without proper garb. He needs you to be the captain, to give clear directions as to what is safe and what is not.

Your child only thinks about his immediate pleasures. For example, he does not want to bathe now. He cannot hold the whole picture of mom, dad, baby and grandparents and all their needs in his head. He will not consider their feelings if dinner is late.

It is up to you, the adult in his life, to see the whole picture and make decisions based on it. Dinner time is dinner time. He can choose between red jelly and orange jelly, but the time of dinner cannot possibly be left up to him.

The idea is to give your child a feeling of empowerment

that is appropriate to her age level. Too much power is not helpful. You, the parent, are your child's chief educator. It is your job to provide her with information about life. She needs to learn good habits like hygiene and eating healthily, giving people space, being considerate of other people's feelings and anger management.

If you teach these behaviors when she is young, she will grow up to feel like a competent and healthy person, which is ideal for self-esteem in the long term. When you are firm, she may resist and be angry and even say she does not like you, but in time she will appreciate your efforts.

There is more to self-esteem than feeling happy in the moment

Other things contribute to building self-esteem and will benefit your child as an adult:

1. Knowing right from wrong

A child needs to know that there is right and there is wrong. When he behaves 'right' he will get affirmations from the people around him and he will feel good about himself. Compare the reactions of your neighbor when your child is rude to her as opposed to being polite to her. The polite behavior will always get a greater reward.

With age, your child will be able to judge his own behavior. When he behaves 'right' he will feel good about himself, but when he behaves badly he will feel guilty, which will undermine his confidence in himself.

2. Relating to others mindfully

When your child learns to be considerate, generous, kind, forgiving, grateful and so on, he will have a map of how to conduct himself in the world. This builds confidence. When he practises these other-centered values, people will love him for it and his confidence will soar sky high.

3. Developing self-mastery

This will be discussed at length in chapter seven.

4. Living life according to a value system

Universal values include: orderliness, cleanliness, personal hygiene, reliability, responsibility, kindness, generosity, striving for excellence, hard work and conscientiousness.

5. Learning to tolerate frustration and delay gratification

These benefits will be fully discussed in chapter six.

Affirmations

Even though you now accept that being firm is helpful to building self-esteem, you will not magically change your ways. Here are some affirmations that you can say to help you feel better about being firm.

Say them even if you do not believe them and they will eventually become part of your way of thinking. Read them and repeat them to yourself so that you can reframe the way you are looking at building self-esteem. You will find your energy levels rising as you take charge and have a direction.

Affirmation 1:

"If I am firm my child will respect me. Commanding respect is an important part of being a parent".

Love and respect are both important aspects of being a parent. I need my child to love me and I love her more than words can say. However, from a child's point of view, respect is equally important. I am her guide and she needs to respect my views and wishes and decisions. I cannot parent effectively without respect. Sometimes I may even choose respect over love.

Affirmation 2:

"Today he is unhappy with my decision but, in the long term, he will love me for teaching him how to behave in the world".

Right now he hates me for not giving in to his demands. As an adult, he will appreciate that I have taught him to delay gratification. As a parent I too need to learn to delay gratification as I will not see the fruits of my labor for many years. My son may not appreciate my efforts until he himself has a child. However, until then, I can feel good about the fact that I am teaching him good life skills. This is my job.

For now, I can bear the discomfort of my child's disapproval. Comfort is a want, not a need. Sometimes in life one has to make uncomfortable decisions for long-term gain. I choose to make decisions that are good for his long-term emotional health rather than a decision based on my need to be liked right now.

Affirmation 3:

"I am the adult in the situation. I have more tools than my child to make decisions about family life".

Sometimes I need to remind myself that I am an adult and not a child playing house. I have responsibilities I need to fulfil. As I am older and wiser than my child, I have the tools necessary to carry out these responsibilities.

I am the captain of this ship and if I need help, I will bring in a competent and experienced navigator, such as my partner or a wise counsellor.

Affirmation 4:

"Children are born to test the limits".

Setting firm limits and giving direction contribute to building self-esteem in a specific manner. Observe children on a playground without a fence. They tend to huddle in the middle. Observe the same group when a fence is erected and you will immediately notice the difference. When there is a fence, children feel secure. They use the whole playground, run all over the place and even try to climb up the fence. They know exactly where they are safe and so feel free to explore, play and exercise.

When they are unsure of the limits (no fence), they tend to restrict themselves in order to feel safe.

Similarly, when your child knows the direction you are moving in, he will be able to join in or test you. However, when one day you are going north (no bath) and the next day you are going south (a bath after an explosion by mom), then your child will feel insecure.

What direction can he test? Do you have a destination? Will you as a family ever get there?

You may find that when you are firm, the initial reaction will be a counter-reaction of pressure. This is normal. It means your child is at the fence, testing how strong it is. If the fence is strong, your child will feel safe to explore his limits. Do not be afraid of the pressure. Stand firm. Reassure your child through your firmness that he is safe. Tomorrow there will be another boundary he will test.

Conclusion

Being firm is a major part of successfully building your child's self-esteem. Children thrive with firm boundaries and a secure, stable parent.

The best thing for my child is for me
to be a wise, firm captain!

Try this:

This week, state calmly what you require. For example: "It is now bath time. Go and have a bath". Use the "tape recorder" method where you repeat this several times without engaging in an argument.

Notice how the number of times you need to repeat yourself decreases each time you stand firm.

If you would like a chart of these affirmations to hang up as a daily reminder, please go to my website **www.parentchildself.com** *and download.*

myth 3

"Quality time means playing a game with my child"

Quality time is a valid concept.

"Quality time" is one of those phrases that caught on like wildfire when it was first introduced. This is because it is a valid concept and reminds parents to interact with their children in a meaningful way.

Today, many parents believe that the only way to achieve quality time with their children is by playing a game with them. This has created extra stress for parents, since finding time to play a game can be extremely difficult. Consequently, it leads parents to make apologies like:

- I know that I should play Lego™ after school with my child but I just have no time.
- I wish I could find time to play a board game with my daughter but afternoons are the time I prepare dinner.

- My wife keeps telling me to wrestle with my son on a Sunday but I just want to relax on the weekend.
- I know it is important for a father to play ball with his son but I am useless at ball games.
- My daughter wants to play house with me but I find I have no patience for it.
- Playstation is a mystery to me. I have no idea how to join in a game.

Put another way, the apologies go something like: "I am sorry that I cannot play the game my child is interested in and I wish I could", or, "I am sorry that I do not have time to play games with my child because life is so hectic". This wish to be someone else; or to be yourself but living a less stressful life; or to be a more available parent hooks in beautifully with the belief, "I must be a perfect parent".

However, it is something more specific than that as well. It is the belief that quality time means joining in with your child at her level, and totally focusing on her wishes.

Lorraine is the mother of a two-year-old boy. She believes that, in order to give her son quality time on an ordinary afternoon, she needs to get on the floor and play Lego™ for a good chunk of time, certainly more than thirty minutes. Lorraine is riddled with guilt because she finds achieving this impossible. She works in her own business and feels stretched for time. Her afternoons and evenings are spent doing housework and catching up on bookkeeping.

Eli is a devoted father. He believes that quality time with his three-year-old daughter should entail reading a book about fairies every day, since fairies are her passion. However, he has a learning disability and struggles to read and so he rarely does. Because of his belief about quality time, Eli is convinced that his daughter is losing out because of his deficiency. He worries that her self-esteem will suffer. He also worries that his long-term relationship with her will be negative because he could not provide adequate quality time when she was growing up.

Both Lorraine and Eli feel bad at not being able to live up to an ideal each of them has taken on board concerning quality time. Feeling guilty creates stress, which lowers energy levels which, in turn, lessens quality time.

Erroneous beliefs about quality time:

- Quality time means total child focus.
- Quality time needs to be set aside for it to happen.
- Quality time can be short but should be daily.
- Quality time is some magical procedure.
- Quality time is essential for building self-esteem.
- Both parents must make time for quality time every day.
- Playing a game is the most effective way of achieving quality time.
- Quality time is a cure-all for many problems.

What really is quality time?

Quality time is an important concept because it highlights the need for busy parents to make time for the emotional needs of their children. It arose when mothers started to work outside of the home and fathers were working longer hours.

The idea of quality time was to stress that, if a parent cannot be with his child all day, he should make the time that they do spend together worthwhile.

Over the years, this concept evolved into meaning that quality time should be worthwhile for the child specifically, and that it was crucial for the development of a healthy self-esteem. Then the concept evolved even further to mean that quality time is best achieved by playing a game of the child's choice every day. This latest interpretation is almost impossible to achieve in today's busy world.

What really is quality time? I define quality time as "time shared between a parent and a child that is meaningful to both". It is possible for a parent and a child to share the same home and have very little quality time. Why? Because the time they spend together is not meaningful or beneficial to either. If a parent does not want to be interacting with the child at that moment, even if physically they are in the same space, then the child will feel distanced, and that cannot be classed as quality time.

Eli, in the example presented above, illustrates this point:

When he tries to read to his daughter, he is uncomfortable. He struggles to read and does not enjoy the activity. Therefore, the time together cannot be regarded as quality time even though Eli hopes it is because his daughter loves to hear about fairies. No matter how pure Eli's intentions, it is not enjoyable for both and therefore is of poor quality.

As a parent, you may feel that the most loving thing you can do is to give your child what she wants. This links to the belief that "in order to build self-esteem, I must be nice all the time". Eli is being exceptionally nice when he tries to give his daughter what she wants. However, his feelings of discomfort will undermine his efforts because she can feel his discomfort and will interpret it to mean that he does not really want to be with her.

> *Lorraine wants to play Lego™ with her son but finds that she gets quite fidgety and distracted when they play. Her mind is somewhere else; she is making plans for her business or deciding on a dinner menu. Her son picks up her emotional absence from the game and does not experience it as quality time.*

What Lorraine and Eli both need to do is find an activity that is meaningful to them as well as to their child. This will ensure that the quality of the interaction is good, and both players are emotionally engaged with one another.

Imagine going ballroom dancing with your partner when she really does not want to be there. Her feet are there but you feel that she is disconnected from you and the activity. She is trying to be nice, and you appreciate it, but the dancing is doing little to bring you closer.

If both partners love to dance and have fun together, they will feel really connected. If dancing does not work, you need to reconsider the activity. If your partner enjoys playing scrabble, and so do you, then quality time is more likely to take place when you play scrabble together.

The purpose of quality time

The purpose of quality time is to nurture a relationship. By embracing the concept of quality time, you are accepting that a relationship needs time. You are also agreeing that the type of time spent together must be special.

What must be remembered is that playing a game your child enjoys is not the only way to achieve this. The key to quality time is to find activities that will truly enhance your relationship with your child.

The secret of true quality time

Your child should feel that you enjoy being with her. The activity that you engage in is of little importance. Strange as it may seem, it truly does not matter what you are doing as long as you are focused on your child.

Aim to achieve the following:

1. Your child feels that you are paying attention to her and that you are not a million miles away.
2. She feels that you are comfortable around her and would not want to be anywhere else.
3. She feels that you are interested in her feelings and wishes and dreams and truly care about her life.
4. She experiences you actively listening to her and responding in an appropriate way.

By thinking this way, you will find that your life is much easier. No longer do you have to turn yourself into somebody you are not. No longer do you have to spend time on activities that you find tiresome.

Good activities to achieve quality time

If you love children's activities like building Lego or finger painting, and so does your child, then go for it. However, if you have limited time or do not enjoy children's games, you will be relieved to know that there are alternative ways to have quality time with your child.

Basically, nearly every time you are with your child, you can create an opportunity for quality time. It is not special time outside of "living"; it is essentially related to the way you interact with one another. You do not need to "make time" for quality time, you simply need to turn everyday activities into a connecting experience.

- When you are driving your child to or from school, turn off your radio and mobile phone. Have a quiet environment and show a willingness to hear what your child has to say. Do not interrogate your child; maybe just ask a general question like: "Did you sleep OK?" or "How was your day?"
- Being in the car together is an excellent time to listen to music you both enjoy. On occasion you can say something like: "That song makes me happy. What about you?"
- Bath time for young children is prime quality time. Taking the opportunity to rub or tickle your child's back and talk about how it feels comprises excellent quality time.
- Bed time is commonly used by parents to connect with their child. Reading is a great way to bond as well as to settle your child for sleep. Questions about how the story made your child feel will enhance her feeling

that you are focused on her and not just getting through the nightly routine.

- Chores are an excellent way of spending quality time with your child. Yes, you read that right. *Chores are an excellent way of spending quality time with your child.* Young children love to help.

  In fact when you push your child away so that you can make dinner, you will cause her to do everything in her power to gain your attention. Rather, involve her in the chore and utilise the time to get to know each other better. It may take longer and it may be messier than if you had done the job alone, but the joy of making scrambled eggs together cannot be beaten (pardon the pun).

  There is always some small job your child can do, no matter how young she is. She can scramble the eggs. She can pass the fork. She can pour the eggs into the pan. As long as she feels that you love having her around, and are focused on what she is doing, you have achieved quality time.

- When you are together, try to minimize distractions. Chat. Chill. Be comfortable together.

Once you master the art of relating to your child through everyday activities, your stress levels will decrease. You will not feel stretched at having to find time for both chores and quality time. You will not feel guilty that the time spent did not involve playing a game. Best of all, your closeness with your child will be enhanced.

Realistic beliefs

The unrealistic beliefs about quality time stated above can now be replaced by more realistic and achievable beliefs:

- I can learn to focus on my child.
- The activity must be enjoyed by both parent and child.
- Quality time can be incorporated into daily life.
- Quality time can be brief.
- Quality time can be long distance.
- Quality time can be placed on hold.
- Quality time contributes only partially to self-esteem.

I can learn to focus on my child

Quality time is not a magical procedure; it is merely spending time with your child and being focused on her. When you give your child your full attention, she will feel that there is nowhere else you would rather be.

The ability to focus is a skill that can be learned. You achieve it by switching off all distractions, not only the radio but the unrelated thoughts in your head. Focus on the stimuli around you: the sights, sounds, tastes, smells and textures in your immediate present.

The activity must be enjoyed by parent and child

Quality time is best achieved when you, the adult, also enjoy the activity. It is very beneficial for your child to feel loved and understood, but in the long term it is equally beneficial for your child to learn that you have feelings and wishes and dreams too. I am not suggesting that you should reveal your secrets or worries to your child. I am talking more about superficial stuff, like taste in music.

> **A practical example:**
> *Play the Wiggles® for your child in the car and ask her how she liked the tune. She may say, "I loved it". Then you can say, "I prefer it when they play fast tunes, I find the slow ones a bit boring".*

This way you and your child can learn about each other's taste in music. More importantly, your child will come to appreciate that you are also a person and have separate tastes and views. As she matures, she will see you as a separate being and not just there to serve her wishes.

Over time your child will learn to consider your taste too. She may say, "This tune is slow. Would you like to skip to a faster one?" Learning to consider the feelings of others is an important relationship skill and plays a huge role in long-term relationships. It will benefit your child enormously.

Quality time can be incorporated into daily life

The possibility of creating quality time comes often during the day. All you need is the awareness to make mental space for your child in your busy day. The more you do it, the more automatic it becomes.

Playing is not the only way you can interact with your child. Reading, cooking, baking, cleaning, driving together, listening to music, doing homework, getting dressed, bathing are all ways of interacting with your child, and it is within your power to make the interaction special.

Quality time can be brief

If you live with your child in the same home, then aim for daily meaningful contact. A short meaningful interaction is better than none, but obviously, if there are many opportunities to share feelings and enjoy activities, then you should grab them. You can never overdose on quality time.

Several brief meaningful moments in a day are much easier to find than thirty minutes or more in a busy afternoon.

Quality time can be long distance

Sometimes daily quality time is not possible. You may be living away from home because of work or a separation. Remember the realistic beliefs of chapter two. Life is not perfect and often sends unexpected difficulties.

The important thing in this case is to keep up as much contact as you can through letters, emails and telephone calls. This will serve to remind and reassure your child that you are thinking of her. When you do speak, focus on your child and show a genuine interest in her feelings and thoughts.

Finally, remember what she says so that the next time you speak, you can show her that you absorbed what she said and made it a part of you.

Example:

Trevor is a construction worker and works on site. Sometimes this means that he is away from his family for a few weeks at a time. He calls every day at the same time so that his daughter feels secure that he will call and that he is thinking about her. He always asks about her day but in a way that shows her that he is linking it to yesterday's conversation or even last week's conversation. He may say, "You told me you were struggling with your painting yesterday. What did your teacher say about it today?"

He may remember that Mondays are netball practice and Tuesdays are violin rehearsals.

Trevor is a good example of a father who is able to make his daughter feel special. By remembering her activities, he demonstrates that he really cares about her daily life. Remembering what she said about her painting yesterday proves to his daughter that he really concentrated on what she said and made a point of remembering it because it was important to her.

Quality time can be placed on hold

Even if you are physically at home, you may be emotionally unavailable for a while during a crisis, such as the death of a parent or spouse. Do not beat yourself up about it. It is all part of the fabric of life and your child will learn about life this way. As long as you have given quality time for the majority of the time, breaks here and there will not do any major damage.

As soon as you feel emotionally ready to give of yourself, then do so. When you explain what happened, your child will feel close to you. By validating his experience that you were absent, you will make him feel noticed, which is a major factor in quality time.

Example:

When Tim lost his job, he could not face his family. He would hang around the house, watching TV and making a few phone calls. He felt that he was not able to play with his son as he was so broken inside. After about a month, he began to feel better about things. As a result, he found the energy to give his son individual attention. When they spent time alone, Tim gave his son the opportunity to talk about how sad he had felt when his dad was sad. These discussions strengthened their relationship enormously.

Quality time only partially contributes to self-esteem

It is true that quality time enhances self-esteem because it makes your child feel valued. However, other things like being firm, communicating effectively, being affectionate and loving unconditionally also have a role to play.

Affirmations

Hopefully, by now you are more relaxed about the concept of quality time and how to implement it. However, old habits die hard and it may be difficult for you to change your behavior initially. Here are some affirmations that you can say to keep your newly learned perceptions uppermost in your mind. Say them often, read them and repeat them to yourself, and they will eventually become part of your way of thinking and will help you change the way you perceive quality time. Not only will you discover that you have more than enough time in the day to have a special relationship with your child, you will have more energy to fulfil your goals.

Affirmation 1:

"When my child is around me physically, I can focus on his emotions".

Any time that we are together I can turn into a meaningful interaction by focusing on her moods and thoughts. Sometimes I will need to make an effort to turn off distracting influences like my mobile phone, or to switch off my racing thoughts. My child's feelings of worth will be enhanced as she realizes that I am prioritizing her over my friends or work.

Affirmation 2:

"Quality time can be built into everyday activities".

I do not have to find a special activity to create quality time. It is lovely to play a game or go on an outing but it is not always possible or realistic. It is just as helpful to incorporate a good emotional experience while carrying out everyday tasks. The added benefit is that my child learns to share my life and begins to understand what adult life consists of. She also learns valuable life skills, like household chores, and the ability to focus on another person.

Affirmation 3:

"Quality time must be meaningful not only to my child but to me as well".

It is a huge relief to learn that I do not have to force myself to engage in activities I do not enjoy. It is also a relief to learn that time spent together is not so much about pandering to my child and giving her a good time, as about nurturing our relationship.

Whilst I realize the importance of focusing on my child's emotions, I do not have to indulge her and give her the impression that it is my job to entertain her. Moreover, when I share some of my tastes and opinions, she can learn to appreciate that other people, including adults, have preferences that need to be considered.

Affirmation 4:

"Quality time can be achieved over the telephone when necessary".

I would love to interact with my child face-to-face every day. Although it is not possible right now, I am not going to beat myself up about it. I will call every day at the same time and make sure I really listen. I will also ensure that I remember little details, like the name of a school teacher or the time of the carnival.

Even if my child finds out that I am writing down the details when she speaks, it will not diminish our quality time. In fact, it may increase her feeling of worth to realize that I am putting in a real effort to remember details of her day.

Conclusion

Quality time can be summed up as time spent with your child that is meaningful and enjoyable to you both. You can have quality time in short spurts during the day, no matter what activity you are involved in. Forget games, forget extended periods of time and forget trying to be who you are not. Be yourself, enjoy your child and interact in real time in real life situations.

Quality time = my child and I together!

Try this:

Today, when you are with your child, be in the moment. Feel pleasure at being together. Then share some of your thoughts and feelings like "I enjoy standing in the sun together, what about you?" Notice how your child's face will light up as he feels you are connecting with him.

If you would like a chart of these affirmations to hang up as a daily reminder, please go to my website **www.parentchildself.com** *and download.*

myth 4
"Parenting must be carried out separately from living an adult life"

Life has become child-focused.

There was a time when being a parent seemed to flow more naturally. You had a child, and life continued much the same, only now there was an extra person to love and to share life's activities with. Thirty years ago it was not uncommon to hear parents brag, "My life is not going to change when this baby is born. He is going to fit right in with our lifestyle".

Nowadays, it is completely different. Parents believe that once you have a child, your life needs to become child-focused. It seems that a parent can have a life but it must be carried out around the activities of the child. Is there any wonder that modern parents feel exhausted? You are exhausted because you are trying to squeeze your busy schedule in "after parenting hours". Your life has become extracurricular to what you view as the central job of caring for your child.

This erroneous belief is closely aligned to the belief that

quality time means playing games with your child and that parent-to-child interaction must be kept separate from parent involvement in adult activities.

Do you do the following?

- Make dinner while your children are watching TV.
- Worry if they are not entertained while you do the laundry.
- Have no adult conversation with your partner while your child is around.
- Limit holiday destinations to places where there are full time child-care facilities.
- Choose holiday resorts where children have a full entertainment schedule.
- Make your child's bed after he goes to school.
- Go shopping while he is at school.
- Stay home rather than go out at night and leave him with a sitter.
- Only socialize with friends who have a child of the same age.
- Give up your hobbies so you can take your child to his extracurricular activities.
- Argue with your partner about who should take the garbage out while your child plays on the computer.

While none of these choices are toxic if done occasionally, they become harmful when done on a regular basis. You see, what you are teaching your child is that:

- His life is the priority.
- Your life is secondary.

- Being responsible and being a child are mutually exclusive.
- You are there to clean up after him.
- Playing is more beneficial than doing a chore.
- Adults and children have little in common.
- Adults and children cannot have fun together unless it is the child's interest that prevails.
- Your child does not have to participate in everyday family life.
- Your child does not have to participate in the running of the household.

Veronica epitomizes these points:

Poor Veronica is worn out from her life with three children. She gets up early to make their school lunches. She then makes sure that they are dressed and ready for school. Sometimes this means searching for the socks she left on the bed the night before and sometimes it means giving the children a drink for breakfast as there is no time for a proper meal.

She throws on a track suit and drives them to school. Only on her return does she shower and change and have a coffee. She would love to study in the mornings but she does not believe it is possible as her mornings are filled with making beds, vacuuming and doing the laundry and ironing. She also prefers to shop for groceries during school hours so that when her kids come home, she is fully available to take them to sport and to do homework.

Veronica cannot fathom why she feels so tired when her days are well organized and the children are well taken care of.

Derek falls into the same category.

> Derek is a sportsman through and through. He loves
> soccer, tennis and squash, and runs every day to keep fit.
> However, his passion is to run a marathon and, for the
> past four years, he has foregone that pleasure. Why?
> Because his four-year-old son has started to learn to play
> soccer and Derek wants to be present at every practice.
>
> If the truth be told, a marathon only occurs every few
> months and Derek would only be missing a practice
> occasionally. However, as a loving dad he thinks that he
> must give up his passion in the interests of his son. Derek
> often feels devastated when he hears about a marathon
> that he will miss out on, but he tries to hide his
> disappointment from his family.

No-one questions Veronica and Derek's love for their children. What I am challenging is the benefit of what they are trying to achieve. By prioritizing his son's sport over his own passion in an ongoing way, Derek is not giving his son the opportunity to learn how to care about another person's interests and needs. Derek is also not being true to himself. This is a recipe for resentment and anger later on.

Derek's son is more than capable of coping if his father misses an occasional practice. He will learn to respect his father's choices and may even learn to reciprocate interest in another person's sport. Derek will feel more fulfilled as a human being and his pleasure will filter down to the whole family.

Simply put, Veronica has become a slave to her children. She believes that by putting out their clothes, making their beds and depriving herself of her early morning coffee, she is doing them a favor. She believes that this is the way to show her love. She has fully embraced the beliefs: "I must be a perfect parent" and "if I am firm I will lower my child's self-esteem".

What Veronica does not realize is that when young children learn life skills, like making a bed and taking out the garbage, they feel wonderful. Their self-esteem soars as they now have a feeling of mastery over their environment. When they contribute to making dinner, they feel proud of themselves, productive and self-satisfied.

When children go shopping with mom, they learn how to follow a list and discover that chores can be fun.

Poor Molly is really struggling:

Molly cannot finish a sentence when her three-year-old, Georgia, is around. When Molly and her husband Greg talk at the end of the day, Georgia interrupts the discussion. She demands milk, or to be picked up, and proceeds to take center stage. Molly worries that if she is firm and insists that her daughter wait her turn, her self-esteem will be negatively affected (see chapter five).

So Molly focuses on Georgia while Greg gets very frustrated with the situation. It goes without saying that their intimate life is also being affected. Molly feels that she has no choice but to continue in this pattern because she brought Georgia into the world and "owes" her. She is prepared to risk her marriage if she has to. This indicates how important Georgia is in her life.

I sympathize with Molly, Greg and Georgia. No-one wins in this scenario even though one would think Georgia would be ecstatic that she has been made such a princess. I feel sorry for Molly because she could lose a marriage over a child who in twelve short years will be running around with her friends, ignoring her mom. I feel sorry for Greg, who wants a marriage, wants an adult relationship with the mother of his child, but whose needs are being disregarded. Most of all, I feel sorry for Georgia, who is missing out on so many good ingredients for a successful life.

It is pretty obvious that if Molly and her husband have a good marriage, Georgia will have a much more secure and happy life than if they split up. The short-term boost to Georgia's self-esteem when she dominates a conversation will disappear if the marriage breaks up. Conversely, she will gain long-term security from being in a happy home.

There are numerous other benefits Georgia would gain should Molly spend some quality time with Greg. The child would learn to wait her turn, to listen to others and to respect their boundaries — all prime factors in successful adult relationships. The immediate benefits would be feelings of safety and security when her parents show firmness and set clear parameters.

Erroneous beliefs about living as a family

- Family life should be child-centered.
- Interaction with your child must be kept separate from doing daily chores.
- Children can learn skills like making a bed at a later stage.
- Your marriage comes second to your children.
- Putting your child's needs first will build his self-esteem.
- Interrupting adult conversation to listen to your child will make him feel important.
- Your child should be made to feel the center of the universe in your family.

- Your child will love you more when you do things for him.
- Other people's ideas about what is good for a child are probably better than yours. For example, the activities provided by a holiday resort must surely be more fun for your child than hiking with you.

Realistic beliefs

Realistic beliefs will free you to lead a more balanced life and will also teach your child to be family-centered.

- Family life does not have to be child-centered.
- Living in a family teaches a child how to live within a community.
- Living in a family teaches your child your values.
- Living in a family teaches your child skills.
- Living in a family teaches your child interpersonal skills.
- It is possible to interact with children and do chores at the same time.
- It is important that you spend some time in the day enjoying your activities.
- When mom and dad prioritize their relationship, the whole family thrives.

Family life does not have to be child-centered

Children are born into a family with a set of parents who had a life before the child was born. Life does not need to end for parents once a child is born. It is healthy for a child to adapt to family dynamics and activities.

While parents need to make some accommodations for a child, it is not necessary to rotate family life totally around the child. Family life can continue and, when necessary, the child comes first. However, there will be many occasions when the needs of the parents will come first.

Lionel demonstrates a sensible approach:

Lionel is very excited because it is his sister's wedding day. However, his excitement is soon marred because his baby has a fever. Lionel and his wife consult with the doctor. The doctor reassures them that it will be fine for them to go to the wedding as long as there is a responsible sitter who will monitor the fever. Lionel decides not to miss this special occasion and the baby is fine, recovering very quickly.

Living in a family teaches a child how to live within a community

A human being is a social animal who lives among other humans. Learning the skills of living in a community comes primarily from family life. In a community, individuals need to know how to share, consider the feelings of others, wait their turn and give back. When a family is child-centered, the child is deprived of opportunities to learn these valuable skills.

Living in a family teaches your child your values

Every family has values it ascribes to. One family believes that it is important in life to fight for what you want, whereas another family believes in choosing the path of peace. One family believes passionately in the value of education, whereas another family believes that working with one's hands is most fulfilling. One family may teach their child about God and another family may teach atheism.

When you focus on your child and change your values in order to placate your child, you are doing him a disservice. He needs to know what you believe so that he can rebel against something (remember the story about the fence around the playground) or comply with a consistent value system.

Trish has taken the path of least resistance:

Trish is an educated woman who worked hard to attain her degrees. She has benefited enormously from her education and thought she would pass on that value to Shana, her daughter. However, now that Shana is ten and wilful, Trish says she finds it exhausting to get Shana to do her homework. She just wants Shana to be happy, and so Trish leaves the topic alone.

My question is: how on earth will Shana ever learn what is important if she is not taught? How will she learn good work ethics with no one to show her? Sensing Trish's distance will only confuse and frighten Shana.

You cannot force your child to follow your value system but you can give him a clear direction in life. He then knows where you stand and feels secure. In 90% of cases, children follow the value system of their parents if they are given one. It may take many years for this to manifest but as a parent you need to keep plugging away if it is something really important to you.

Living in a family teaches your child skills

When families interact, all kinds of skills are passed down. You learnt your mother's pasta recipe by interacting, not by formal teaching. You learnt how to change a light bulb by helping dad. Without even realizing it, when you were around your parents, you absorbed many practical skills.

In today's scenario, how can your child learn a skill if you send him to watch TV while you change the light bulb? How can your child learn to make a bed if you do it while he is at day care? How can he learn to beat an egg if you never give him an egg and a fork and let him experiment?

It is vital, in a practical way, for your child to participates in your activities according to the boundaries you set for him. This will ensure many life skills when he is an adult.

Living in a family teaches your child interpersonal skills

The family is the preparation ground for the world. The more good exposure your child receives at home, the easier she will cope with the big world out there. Learning values like right and wrong will go a long way to helping her live a moral life. This in turn will gain her respect and happiness.

Learning practical skills will assist your child to feel competent in the world. It is a great feeling to be able to knead dough at school well because at home you helped with the baking. It is satisfying to know how to tidy up after yourself, plus get the approval of your teacher for doing so.

Besides values and skills, family life prepares you for successful long-term relationships. When your child learns to consider others by allowing you to speak to your partner, he will be a good friend to others as he will give them space to speak. When your child learns to wait his turn, he will be welcomed into a group as he knows how to be a team player.

When your child is happy to participate in your activity, he will be happy to participate in his friend's activities as well.

As an adult, these skills are invaluable in contributing to a sustainable long-term partnership.

It is possible to interact with children and do chores at the same time

As much as possible, you should try and involve your child in everyday activities. You now know that this is a valuable form of quality time and will build your child's self-esteem immeasurably. In my opinion, it is preferable for your child to wake up half an hour earlier to make his own bed before leaving for school, than making it yourself when he is gone. Even a two-year-old can help as you pull up his doona.

It is important that you spend some time in the day enjoying your own activities

When you do tasks while your child is at home and you receive assistance, you will be freed up to do other activities. As a stay-at-home mom, you may want to do yoga in the mornings or meet a friend for coffee. As a working mom, you may want to spend time on the weekends doing yoga or meeting friends or even sleeping in. As a working dad, you could go for a run on a Sunday morning or invite a mate over for a beer.

When you engage in the activities you have always enjoyed, you will feel energized. This will have a positive impact on your child as you will be a more loving and patient parent. There is no reason that your child cannot come and watch you do yoga or play quietly while you talk to a friend.

When mom and dad prioritize their relationship, the whole family thrives

I cannot emphasize this point enough. When you neglect your marriage, you are doing your child a disservice. Your child will thrive in a happy home. He will revel in the security that comes with having parents who love each other. And equally important — *for you are no less important than your child* — you will be happy.

A couple needs to nurture their relationship if it is to survive in the long term. When children leave home a vacuum can be created, and if the relationship between you and your partner has been child-centered, you will find you have no relationship left. Also, if your relationship is strong while your child is growing up, it will be a major source of support for you.

Raising a child is tough at times. Difficult decisions have to be made, firm resolutions have to be kept, and your child is powerful. When you stand together with your partner, it is that much easier to withstand the power of your child's resistance. When you feel loved and supported by your partner, you will be a more loving and content parent.

Make time to be together. Go on dates. Laugh. Use the same principles given for quality time with your child in your marriage. Focus on each other. Care about each other's feelings, dreams and aspirations and not just about getting through the daily grind.

Affirmations

I hope you are now excited about the prospect of having an adult life while being a parent. Since old beliefs have a way of

CHAPTER FIVE — PARENTING IS SEPARATE

staying put, practising a new way of thinking is imperative. By articulating the affirmations below, you will soon translate the theory into practical reality.

Affirmation 1:

"I must nurture my marriage while parenting".

I am not detracting from my child when I make quality time for my marriage; I am actually enhancing my child's life by providing a happy home, love, security and a two-parent household.

Affirmation 2:

"Working together as a family is enriching".

When I am busy making dinner and my child is watching TV, there is no benefit either way. However, when he helps me, we can have quality time. He also learns skills and I receive welcome assistance.

When we do an activity together it is an opportunity for me to teach him values, like the importance of tidiness or of eating vegetables. Social skills like learning to collaborate, are intrinsic to working this way.

Affirmation 3:

"I can enjoy my life as a parent".

My child can enhance my life, not detract from it. When I enjoy my life and include my child in it, she blossoms. When I ensure that she has enough child activities, she will also blossom. The balance is to have my activities, her activities and shared activities. Sharing our lives makes us happy and takes the load off my shoulders a lot of the time.

Affirmation 4:

"For him to be happy I do not need to pander all day to my child's wishes".

Knowing this brings great relief. It was so exhausting thinking of activities he would enjoy while trying to fit in things I needed to do. Also, I had to stretch myself to find the time, the money and the energy to get him to an activity. Now I know he can be happy just being with me or doing an everyday task. Also this will build his self-esteem and feelings of security.

Conclusion

Life after the birth of your child *does* exist. You can have a full and enjoyable life as an adult and be a great parent. In fact, you will be a better parent when you feel fulfilled and happy in your marriage, social life and the way you run your home. Your child is a huge part of your life and you can really enjoy each other, but not to the exclusion of the rest of your life.

A good parent can be a fulfilled adult, too!

Try this:

Make a date with your partner. Tell your child on the day that you are going out. No matter your child's reaction, stay firm, state that it is your time and that you need adult time. Watch how your child thrives knowing that you and your partner's relationship is secure.

If you would like a chart of these affirmations to hang up as a daily reminder, please go to my website **www.parentchildself.com** *and download.*

myth 5

"My child must have every material benefit in order to be happy and successful"

Consumerism is all-consuming.

Since the Second World War, the Western world has been focused on building material wealth. Perhaps it is a reaction to the Great Depression and the horrors of war. Whatever the reasons, it has become a value system that has infiltrated every facet of our daily lives. Working hard to make a dollar is the driving force,. Family time has been diminished to a few hours a day or a few weeks a year.

Living simply has become a thing of the ancient past. Now individuals long for more and more material possessions. We are obsessed by consumerism. Our three-year-old car, which still drives perfectly, is no longer acceptable; we need to buy a new one with brand new features. Our computer still fulfils its functions but, according to the latest adverts, it is slow (by milliseconds) and needs to be replaced. Our mobile phone is only one-year-old and without a scratch, but we believe we must upgrade to a slimmer model with extra features.

What are we really telling ourselves when we have the urge to upgrade our possessions?

We are telling ourselves that:

- New is better than old.
- Being up-to-date with the latest will make us happy.
- Having the best of everything shows that we are successful.
- We cannot possibly be happy if we just chug along with our basic needs met.
- Possessions bring happiness.
- Making money is the most important thing in life.
- Success is measured by our bank balance.
- Our material wants must be satisfied ASAP.
- External objects can make us happy internally.
- We are deprived if we have less than others.
- Being deprived of a toy is a crisis.
- Keeping up with the Joneses is important.

The consequences of materialism

What is the result of this thinking? The EBB FLOW model introduced in Chapter One teaches us that these beliefs will drive certain behaviors. These behaviors are easy to identify in our culture. Does the following sound familiar?

- You work very hard to earn enough to satisfy the material needs of your family.

- You work even harder when you want to increase your material comforts.
- You spend less time on your marriage than you would like, because work is paramount.
- You spend a limited amount of time with your children, because you need to earn more money to buy them things.
- You worry that you are not successful enough.
- You feel a failure as a parent because you cannot provide your child with every possession his heart desires.

Perhaps you are reading this and saying to yourself, "This does not pertain to me. I am not that materialistic". You do not have to be materialistic to be bound by these beliefs. On a subtle level, without even knowing it, you may well be caught up in the belief that supplying your child with all his material needs will give him happiness.

The following questions will give you clarity on your position in this matter:

- Have you ever felt sorry that you were not able to buy your child the latest Nintendo?
- Have you ever felt guilty that you were not able to afford private schooling for your child?
- Do you ever worry about how your child will feel when he brings friends home to your very ordinary house?
- Do you ever dream of winning the lottery just so you can take your child on an overseas trip?
- Have you ever apologized to your child for going on a caravan holiday instead of going to a fancy hotel?

- Have you ever confided to your spouse that you feel like a failure because you are not able to buy your child designer clothes?
- Have you ever implied that your partner is a failure because you are not able to afford designer clothes for your child?
- Do you ever go without something you really need, like a new suit for work, so that you can have a birthday party for your child at an expensive venue?
- Have you ever gone into debt in order to buy a gadget for your child which, in retrospect, he hardly ever used?

Most modern parents have these worries because they have internalized the erroneous belief that their child will be happier if she has every material wish fulfilled. Advertising experts hone in on this belief, bombarding you with adverts that say you will be really happy and fulfilled when you buy this house/dress/mobile phone/plasma TV/car etc. Actually, whatever I have written here will be outdated by the time you read this, so please just insert the most fashionable objects of the time!

The point I am trying to make remains the same, however, no matter the actual material object. The advert for the product is there to convince you that no matter how happy you think you are now, you will be so much happier if you buy the product.

No wonder it feels so hard to be a parent today! You have to work so hard to make a living but you can never relax and feel you have "arrived". For example, there was a time when the goal in society was clear and defined: buy your own home and pay it off as quickly as possible. This meant that by 'forty something' you could relax. Modern society tells you to upgrade continuously. Therefore, you move several times in twenty years to more expensive homes, which results in there being no end point for payment. Instead, each move results in an increase of expenses, which brings increasing work pressures.

Added to this are other pressures: to upgrade furniture, appliances, and entertainment, for example. The end result is that you are tired, stressed, cash-strapped and (surprise, surprise) not happy. You have found out the hard way that the "American Dream" does not bring happiness. It brings material comfort and status, but these do not necessarily contribute to happiness in life. In fact the American Dream has actually become a nightmare for many people.

> *Aileen is an interior designer who was determined to open her own store. Eventually she did so, at great emotional and financial cost. She hired a nanny to take care of her children, reassuring herself that they were well taken care of.*
>
> *Every time a new fashionable lamp or bed cover came on the scene, Aileen proudly redecorated her children's rooms. She felt she was serving them well; they just wanted her to read them a story.*

How to acquire happiness

Happiness has nothing to do with material possessions or fancy holidays or beautiful homes but everything to do with warm relationships, positive attitudes and living with a good moral code. Rich people are not happier than middle class people. The man driving the latest sports car is no jollier than the guy driving the sedan. The family living in the fancy house at the beach is just as troubled as the family living in a semi on a busy road.

Cast your mind back to a time when you really wanted something material and then you got it. Perhaps it was a new sofa or a new phone. You might remember being excited and happy for a few days, and then life just slipped back to the way it was before. You reverted to your old complaints about your life, and soon found something else to dream about.

That is what happens with material possessions. They give short-term satisfaction, and when we become accustomed to them we move on to wanting something else. The same applies when you give something new and flashy to your child. She is excited for a short time and then it is no big deal. She may even stop playing with it after a few hours and hardly go back to it. Buying her that flashy toy did nothing for her long-term happiness in life.

There are a lot of other things you can do to ensure that your child will be happy in the future. Please read this carefully because I stress the word 'future' as opposed to being happy in the here and now.

Sometimes, as a parent, we have to make decisions that will not make our child happy now, but in the future will bring her long-term happiness. For example, if you insist that your child does her homework every day, she may grumble and rather be playing outside. However, when she gets good grades she will feel good about herself. When she lands a good job as an adult as a result of her good grades, she will have self-fulfilment on a daily basis.

Realistic Beliefs

Societal beliefs have a huge influence on our daily choices but it is imperative not to buy into these beliefs just because they are fashionable. There are other beliefs more realistic and helpful that will set the stage for a happier life:

- Wants are not needs. We can live without fulfilling our wants.
- Becoming rich is not completely in your hands.
- Pleasures are short-lived, gratifications last forever.
- Relationships are the main source of happiness.
- Living a life of meaning guarantees happiness.
- Following values in life promotes happiness.
- Thinking positively is what creates happiness.

Wants are not needs — we can live without having wants fulfilled

Every family has basic material needs that must be met to function adequately. Basic needs are things like food, clothing, shelter, warmth and a comfortable bed. Over and above basic needs, most material possessions can be regarded as luxuries. In modern times, one does not hear the word luxury very much because we are persuaded by sellers that each product is a necessity.

When you have a limited budget, think about whether what you are buying is a want or a need.

- Your child has four pairs of shoes. Does she really need a fifth pair?

- Your child has a PlayStation with lots of games. Does she really need to change to an Xbox now?
- Your child needs a new jumper. Does it have to be a designer brand or will buying from a store like Target provide a warm, attractive jumper that will not break the bank?
- You go out for a meal. After the meal your child demands lollies. Does she really need them?
- Your child has a comfortable bed with attractive linen. She says she wants different linen with her favorite superhero as the design. You know she will outgrow this phase soon. Will she benefit in any way from the new linen? Can your budget afford to pay for a short-term phase?

Becoming rich is not completely in our hands

There is an unrealistic belief that if we really try hard enough, each one of us can definitely be a millionaire. No wonder we work harder and harder — we are driven by an untruth. The truth is that you cannot guarantee you will be rich no matter how hard you work.

In chapter two, we talked about how life presents many challenges and unexpected surprises. In the money arena it becomes very obvious that this is so. Think of people you know who were making a good living and then, out of the blue, they lost their job, the stock market crumbled, property prices dropped, or their new business failed.

It may even have happened to you. You may have been doing well in the money stakes and then a competitor drove business away from your store; your superannuation fund went broke, causing you to lose your retirement fund; or the money you made had to be spent on medical treatment for a sick child. The list is endless as life seems to have an inexhaustible supply of original ideas to help you lose your money.

The opposite is also true. Sometimes, people who do not work hard or who are no cleverer than you seem to hit the jackpot. For instance, do you remember the class clown whom you thought would never amount to much? Well, her uncle employed her and she earns an executive salary. Also, the poor family down the road won the lottery and your friend's crazy idea took off. Perhaps it even happened in your life. You may have stayed in your job during tough times and then your company merged with a larger company and you got a raise, or perhaps you took an option in a small business years ago and today your gamble has paid off.

What is in our hands is to work hard, try our best and live within our means. We can be happy without being millionaires and so can our children. Teaching them to work hard, to be honest and to appreciate what they do have will guarantee their happiness in later life. This will help more than leading them on in the belief that they too must bust their guts to be rich at all costs.

Pleasures are short-lived, gratifications last forever

Seeking pleasure is a natural thing. However, in modern times seeking pleasure has become predominant, to the exclusion of other behaviors. More and more people are making choices that provide instant gratification and instant pleasure rather than holding out for more meaningful and long-term gains.

You need to know that when you teach your child to hold on for long-term gains, you will be shaping a happy future. This ability to delay gratification means learning to wait for the reward and the wait is certainly worth it.

Another ability your child will learn is the ability to tolerate frustration. Life is full of frustration, and coping with it leads to a happier life. Being forever upset by everyday inconveniences is a recipe for unhappiness, and no amount of material wealth will change that.

As your child's chief educator, you have many opportunities to teach her these abilities. Know that you are doing her a favor and not depriving her of anything of real value when you say no to a transient, meaningless trinket. Here are some common scenarios that will arise and that you can capitalize on (pun intended) to teach your child valuable life skills which equate with happiness:

- Your child wants red lollies. You know that they will rot her teeth and therefore say "no". She screams at you, feeling hard done by. As a teenager, however, she will have great satisfaction when she is admired by the orthodontist and her peers for having beautiful teeth.
- After dinner, your child wants to run around. You believe that it is important for him to help clear away the dishes. He argues and cries but you insist and he grudgingly complies, believing that he has missed out on free time. When he is living his own independent life as an adult in later years, he will recognize that this helpful behavior he learned as a child has assisted greatly in his transition from living at home with family, to living and looking after himself.

- Reading is difficult for your child. She would rather watch TV. You persist in making her practise her reading. She resents you for making life so hard. However, later in life when she works as a successful barrister, she will gain much satisfaction from being able to read long legal documents.

- You do not have the money to buy an iPod for your child. You tell her that she can save for it with her pocket money and you will match her savings for her birthday present. Your child says you are mean and that all her friends who have iPods have nicer parents. As a young adult, however, she will feel gratified that she is able to budget and work for the things she desires. She will be financially responsible, which will result in few financial worries and an overall sense of accomplishment.

Relationships are a major source of happiness

Whereas a rich person is not necessarily a happy person, research has shown that having a loving family and good friends is a major source of happiness. Therefore, when you give your child quality time by focusing on him (see chapter four), he will feel really content with life. Also, when you are loving and affectionate towards him, he will feel true joy.

Unlike becoming rich, which is not completely in your hands, building successful relationships *is* very much up to you. Making time to be with your family and showing love and affection is entirely in your control. Moreover, developing meaningful friendships will enrich your life, and the life of your child, in multiple ways.

It is worth remembering:

- Instead of feeling bad that you cannot buy the latest digital camera for your child, spend the day at the beach with her making a memory she will never forget.
- Instead of working longer hours to pay for tuition your child does not need, spend those hours teaching him about life and relationships.
- Instead of wishing that you were in a fancy hotel where dinner is served, show your child how much fun it is to cook dinner under the stars.

Money cannot buy a loving moment. As an old man, your child will not remember the new bed linen you slaved for when he was four. He will remember the hugs under the doona when you put him to sleep.

Living a life of meaning guarantees happiness

We all yearn for meaning and value in our lives. When a person can attribute meaning to an event, she will feel content. Even if the event is an unhappy one, if meaning can be found, the event will feel manageable.

Compare the reactions of Lucy and Jane:

Lucy is an unhappy woman. She feels let down by life because she lost the job that she had held for the past ten years. She believes that she gave of her best and was not appreciated. She cannot let go of her negative thoughts and feelings and is finding it difficult to move on and find another job.

Jane is in a similar position to Lucy. She too lost her job after a decade. However, Jane feels pretty upbeat because she believes that losing her job was part of Life's Plan for her. She believes that she needed to be pushed to start her own business and that she would never have had the courage to do so if she still had her job. By attributing meaning to her job loss, Jane feels optimistic about her life and is able to push forward and meet life's challenges.

Having a purpose in one's life is an important way of making life meaningful. For example, a teacher who believes that her input is invaluable to young children will feel needed and happy. A nurse who does not earn very much, but knows that every day she makes her patients comfortable, will feel good about herself. Volunteers for charities who are trying to alleviate the suffering of others feel pretty content because they know that they are making a difference in the world.

Example:

Celeste is a teacher at the same school as Barbara. Celeste wakes up every morning dreading her day. She resents her work because she earns an average salary, which she thinks is not a reflection of the amount of work she puts in. Every time a student asks for help, she gets more miserable as she feels that she is being taken for granted.

Barbara, on the other hand, does not think too much about her salary. She would love to earn more, of course, but accepts that teachers earn an average salary. However, on a daily basis she is excited by her work as she believes that by educating young people, she is making a meaningful contribution to the future.

Teaching your child that a life of meaning is what promotes happiness is one of the greatest treasures that you can give her. At every opportunity you can be a role model and convey this principle. For example, when you experience a crisis like losing your job, you can talk about how it is part of Life's Plan for you and the family.

When your child does not get accepted for a cricket team, spend time looking for lessons that she can learn from this letdown. Allow her to work out that perhaps she needed to learn humility, or perhaps she should spend more time with her musical pursuits. When she moans about having to do a chore, remind her how she is helping the family and making a meaningful contribution to everyone's life.

Following values in life promotes happiness

Living by an ethical value system is a great source of well being. When you value things like honesty, hard work, kindness, persistence, diligence, responsibility and live by these values, every day you will feel good. We human beings automatically feel good about ourselves when we do the right thing. When you teach your child these values, then feeling good about herself can occur on a daily basis. These good feelings will endure and become a permanent part of your child's self-esteem.

Children have no problem understanding there is a right way to behave and a wrong way to behave. Perhaps it sounds politically incorrect for me to say this in a generation where anything goes. However, no matter how much society says that any behavior is basically acceptable, individuals feel guilty and despairing nonetheless. You know what I mean. Let us say that you lied to your child about something. It does not sit comfortably with you. You know that what you did was wrong. Relationships should be based on honesty, a universal value.

Every day your child can feel good about not stealing, lying or hurting someone. She will also feel really good about herself when she is kind, generous, reliable, honest and brave. When she is an adult, she can continue to live by these values which will guide her in her decisions and result in overall happiness.

Example:

Rafael had a wonderful opportunity to get rich quick. He worked at a bank and had access to clients' account numbers. All he had to do was supply an acquaintance of his with those numbers. He did not actually have to steal. He would not even know what amounts were taken from whom.

Rafael's wish to be rich was stimulated and he saw numerous ways he could spend the money to help others. Then he asked himself how he would feel after he did it. He knew he would feel rotten and guilty and wicked. He therefore declined the "offer to help" and even though he had not acquired material riches, he acquired peace of mind.

When you internalize the belief that it is by adhering to an ethical value system that you will find inner contentment, you can teach your child this essential principle. Together you can accumulate a bank balance of good deeds. Even a small child can feed a pet, visit a sick grandparent or help a needy classmate. You will be amazed at how accomplished and happy your child will feel on a daily basis.

Thinking positively is what creates happiness

Material possessions are external, whereas thoughts are internal. We cannot always buy what we want but we can always choose our thoughts. Remember the EBB FLOW model from chapter one. It states that what you *think* determines how you *feel* and *behave*. When you choose positive interpretations of events, you will feel happy. Negative interpretations will result in unhappiness.

Every day you have opportunities to teach your child how to think differently. When you hear him voice a negative view about something, turn it into a positive. However, if he is very distressed, it is not a good time to try and change his thinking. Wait until he has calmed down (even if it is the next day) and then talk about it and offer alternative ways of viewing things.

Examples:

Every time Yolanda woke up to rainy weather, she complained that her day was ruined as she could not swim or play outside. Her mother decided to actively educate Yolanda about the benefits of rain. When Yolanda grasped it, she felt good about "giving up" her pleasure to benefit her mother's garden.

When Yves would complain that his friends let him down by not coming to play at his house, his father would point out the benefits of having time to play alone and be creative. After several months, Yves began to see that each situation had merit and he felt more satisfied with his social life.

Affirmations

Here are some affirmations that will help you to challenge the belief that material possessions will make your child happy. Say them over and over to yourself, and aloud in the presence of your child, until you actually believe them. When you find yourself doubting them because of societal pressure, re-read this chapter and say the affirmations repeatedly until you feel settled again.

Affirmation 1:

"This item is a want, not a need".

My child really does not need this "thing". He will be no happier in the long term if I buy it for him. He will gain much more from learning to live without luxuries and learning to tolerate frustration.

Affirmation 2:

"If I feed consumerism, it will grow and grow".

The more one buys, the more one wants. Therefore, if I stop buying wildly and only buy what I need, I will curb the urge to spend. Similarly, if my child learns not to "need" everything she sees, in the long term she will not want as much.

Affirmation 3:

"Pleasure is short-lived and gratification lasts forever".

When I cave into my child's demands for this toy, he will be happy for a short while and then it will pass. When he learns to work for the toy, the joy he will get from accomplishing something will impact on him for the rest of his life.

Affirmation 4:

"I feel good about teaching my child how to acquire true happiness".

Instead of feeling guilty that I am not rich and cannot buy my child every luxury, I feel really pleased that I can offer other things like love, friendship, and support. Money cannot buy love or happiness, but love can bring happiness. Similarly, teaching my child that life has meaning gives her the option of lasting happiness regardless of her external circumstances.

When I educate my child to live a life by a moral code, she will have self-respect and dignity which, in turn, result in a happy life.

Affirmation 5:

"Positive thoughts produce happiness".

External factors do little to create a happy life. Learning how to see everyday situations in an optimistic way breeds contentment. I cannot control the external factors in my child's life but I can teach her how to think in a positive way. That makes me feel that I am a good parent.

Conclusion

Money does not necessarily buy happiness. Living a life of meaning, enjoying good relationships, aspiring to good values and learning to think independently are what ensure a contented life. All these factors are within your reach and you can teach them all to your beloved child.

A life rich in love will make my child happy!

Try this:

When your child seems unhappy, do not rush out to buy the latest gadget. Rather, allow the feeling and find an emotional tool to sooth the hurt. For example, when your child says that his friend has an electric mixer, make up a hilarious game utilising your hand mixer. Monitor how quickly your child forgets her unhappiness.

Why must he struggle with a knife and fork when I can do it so easily for him?

myth 6

"I must do everything for my child so that he will feel good about himself and feel safe in the world"

Comfort is the goal

Modern parents are worriers. They worry about being the perfect parent. They worry about their child in every way. Is he safe? Is he happy? Is he busy? Is he comfortable?

The underlying beliefs driving the worry are:

- For my child to be happy, he must be comfortable at all times.
- If he is protected from hardship of any sort, he will feel good about himself.
- If I make his life easy for him, he will know that I love him.
- Life should be easy.
- Life should be comfortable.
- Hardships are bad.
- The world is not a safe place.

- Struggle is bad.
- Feeling good at all times is the most important thing.
- Success should happen without much effort.
- An easy life is a happy life.
- My child will learn by osmosis simply by watching me do the job.
- The way to show love is to do things for my child.
- My child will learn life skills just by growing older.

Comfort has become a goal of modern society. It seems that we have come to view an "easy life" as the good life and hard work as an unfortunate necessity for the unlucky few. This has led us to strive for ease and to resent hard work. As a parent you may have found that you feel pity for your child when he has to work hard at something.

The "Microwave Age"

Not only has comfort become important in our generation, but so has speed. Our modern society has been called the "microwave age", where everything is expected to happen quickly and without effort. Remember when it took three hours for a roast? Well, today you can place raw meat and vegetables into a microwave in the morning, set the dial, and have a piping hot meal ready for you when you arrive home at the end of the day.

While technology has enabled many things to be achieved at a high speed, development of the human being still needs time and effort. It is not possible for a child to learn a skill if somebody is doing it for him. It is not possible for a child to learn a skill without repetition and practice. It is not possible to learn a skill without some discomfort.

You may be mentally challenging what I am saying, thinking: "I don't do everything for my child". While that may be true, you may inadvertently ascribe to the above belief and demonstrate it in your behavior.

Do any of the scenarios below ring a bell for you?

- You dress your four-year-old in the morning because it is just easier for everybody.
- Your two-year-old wants to buckle her shoe but you do it yourself as you cannot bear to wait while she struggles with the clasp.
- When your eight-year-old has a project to do, you handle the detailed bits yourself as you feel it is too hard for him, and you want him to do well.
- Your one-year-old likes to feed herself but you insist on feeding her because you cannot bear to watch her find her mouth with messy fingers.
- Your seven-year-old likes to bake. You tell her she can learn to bake when she is big, but for now, she only has to worry about having fun.
- After shopping, you carry all the bags inside and let your child run off and play. You feel he is still young and does not need to be burdened with chores
- Your six-year-old has a friend over to play. They leave a huge mess in your lounge room. You dutifully clean it up. After all, your child is only six and has many years ahead of her to do housework.
- Football is important to your nine-year-old son. He really wants to make the team but the coach said that he will need to practise very hard to improve his kick. You move your son to another football club because you feel that the coach has not valued your son enough.

- Five is a crucial age to learn to read. Your daughter needs to practise every day to keep up with the class, which she is perfectly able to do. However, you want to speed up the process, so you hire a tutor to read with her every day.

In all these scenarios, the child has been deprived of the struggle. Yes, I said *deprived* because when a child struggles and learns and eventually succeeds, his life is enriched. In short, struggling is enriching.

Realistic beliefs

Several realistic beliefs will assist you to be more relaxed about your parenting tasks:

- The natural cycle of life entails struggling.
- Success comes from hard work and sweat.
- Early struggles make it easier to cope later.
- Hard work brings the reward of self-satisfaction.
- Mastery builds self-esteem.
- Skills for independence help to cope in the real world.

The natural cycle of life entails struggling

No matter how hard you try, you will not get away from the struggles life brings. They are guaranteed. No-one you know has had a life free of struggles. I am not even talking about major difficulties like health issues, relationship breakdowns or financial hardships. They certainly exist in the fabric of life, but I am talking about the ordinary process of living day-to-day.

Example:

Tali grew up in a home where her parents argued. They were basically happy together but seemed to have conflict over little things, such as where to go on holiday. Tali promised herself that she would have a conflict-free marriage.

Now that Tali has been married for three years she has come to understand how hard it is for a couple to live together and agree on things. Even in good marriages work needs to be done to solve problems together.

Tali realizes now that relationships cannot be smooth all the time and at times there will be difficulties to overcome.

She is grateful that she saw her parents argue and resolve their differences, as now that she is an adult, she knows that conflict is normal and that her marriage is not on the rocks.

Success comes from hard work and sweat

Every successful person I have met has told me about the hard work they had to put into becoming a success, often over decades. My endocrinologist studied for fifteen years before he could treat me privately. My neighbor, a talented violinist, practises for several hours every day. Biographies of successful business people all highlight the initial struggle and hard work to reach the top.

Early struggles make it easier to cope later

When you teach your child that struggling is bad and hard work should be the exception, it will be much harder for him when he faces a challenge. Simply put, if your child learns that struggling with life's challenges is normal, it will be easier for him to move forward. If he grows up being used to putting in effort in order to succeed, he will be better equipped to cope with adult demands.

Rubin struggled with maths. He desperately wanted to become a dentist and knew that maths was a requirement at university. His entire high school life was consumed with maths, as he put in every effort to succeed. Eventually he was accepted to dental school and he was thrilled that his hard work had paid off.

His friend Jeff had no problems at school but, when he started university, he found it hard to keep up with everybody. Suddenly effort was required and he was floundering. He remembered how Rubin had put in the hours and he realized that he would have to do the same if he wanted good results. Jeff could not avoid the struggle, it just came at a later date. Rubin, on the other hand, had less difficulty adjusting to university demands as he had learned good work habits in high school.

Hard work brings the reward of self-satisfaction

While society is promoting the idea that "an easy life is a happy life", it creates the impression that the opposite must be true, namely, that "a life filled with hard work is an unhappy life". In my experience, this is not necessarily so. In fact, I have found that hard work can even promote happiness. Enduring happiness has been demonstrated to result from being in the "zone" that hard work creates. The "zone" is a mental space where you are busy, focused, fulfilled and feeling productive.

Saul loves to build things. When his father supplies him with wood, nails and a few tools, he immediately gets to work. The whole afternoon can pass before he realizes, and afterwards he feels really happy.

His father understands the feeling because, as an engineer, he has opportunities to get into "the zone". No matter how challenging a project, when he has spent hours focused on planning and problem-solving, he feels invigorated, not tired. That is why he encourages his son to spend his afternoon working on a task rather than just hanging around.

Your child will benefit when you allow him to achieve things on his own. When you finish the detail for your son's project, for instance, he may feel loved and even relieved at being saved the effort, but he will not have a feeling of ownership over the outcome. Even if he gets a good grade, in his heart it will not seem like an accomplishment because he knows that he did not do it all himself.

However, if you let him complete the project in his own way, he will experience feelings of independence, ownership and confidence, which will boost his self-esteem. Moreover, the next time a similar challenge presents itself, he will feel confident to forge ahead.

Mastery builds self-esteem

It is not just the effort that brings satisfaction, it is the sense of mastery, the realisation that "I can do this". Money cannot buy that. When your child struggles to buckle her shoe and finally succeeds, she feels accomplished. She has mastered a new skill. She realizes that she has enough finger dexterity to achieve her goal. No amount of praise can substitute for the wonderful feeling of mastery.

Example:

Debbie is a teenager who loves to run. When she turned fifteen, she set herself the goal of getting in shape and finishing a half marathon. She worked very hard to reach her goal. She trained in the early hours of the morning so that her school work would not be affected. She avoided all the sugary food presented at her friends' parties. She cancelled certain late night social arrangements because she needed to wake up early.

Her friends teased her and, at times, she did feel deprived. However, when she completed the race, her happiness was immense. Her feelings of achievement were huge as she realized what obstacles she had overcome. She knew that no sweets or sleep-ins could have given her the joy she experienced when she succeeded. Moreover, for the rest of her life, she could tap into those good feelings whenever she needed to.

Skills for independence help to cope in the real world

When a child is not afraid to be independent, he copes much better with adult life. For some reason not known to me, parents of today protect and, dare I say, overprotect their children. Perhaps it is because there is more crime and danger today. Or perhaps parents are trying so hard to be perfect that they leave no space for their child to grow.

Mimi exemplifies over-protection:

Mimi loves her daughter, who is six years old. She likes to show her love in many different ways, such as cutting up her food, dressing her in the morning, staying with her at a friend's birthday party and spending large amounts of time at school watching her daughter interact with other children.

In my opinion, Mimi is doing too much for her child and is not giving her space to grow as an individual. A child has a natural urge to be independent but is afraid of it, resulting in an ongoing dependence-independence struggle between parent and child. This struggle starts around two years of age and is in full measure in adolescence.

Here is a typical example of the struggle:

Mom: *"Darling, I want you to wear your blue jumper."*
Son: *"NO!"*
Mom: *"But, darling, it is cold outside."*
Son: *"NO!"*

This kind of argument can go on and on, and as all parents know, the two-year-old often wins. There is no logic involved; the two-year-old simply wants to state that he is an independent being with his own opinions. This is a good thing. As a caring parent you want your child to be independent someday, so the best way of handling this is to allow as many decisions as possible to be made by the child. We call this offering a limited choice.

Mom: *"Darling, choose what jumper you want to wear."*

> Son: *"I want the red one."*
> Mom: *"That's a good choice."*

When the two-year-old feels that he has a choice, there will be less conflict. Mom knows that a jumper is necessary, but what color it is makes no difference in the scheme of things. The amount of choice offered increases with age. Children need to be encouraged to make choices about things like friendships and excursions.

> *Mom to four-year-old daughter:*
> > *"Darling, Mary has asked you to her party on Saturday. Would you like to go?"*
> *Daughter: "No! She is mean to me."*
> Mom: *"That's okay, sweetheart. It is not essential to go."*

Children thrive when they have choices. However, if the choice is life-threatening (wearing summer clothes in the snow), significant in the scheme of things (granny will be devastated if he does not come), or dangerous in any way to the child (going door-to-door to collect money), you should override it.

The truth about feeling safe

In my experience as a clinical psychologist, I have found that when a parent does too much for her child, the child does not necessarily feel safe in the world. In fact, over-concern may even contribute to her feeling frightened a lot. Sometimes, the child may start to feel safe only when the parent is around, causing clingy or dependent behavior. Sometimes you may not be aware that there is a problem until your child has to face a challenge and cannot cope with it.

The truth is that children who have made independent decisions from an early age and have learned to do things for themselves have the best chance of feeling safe in the world. Why? Because the world is not a puzzle to them. They have the skills that help to face life's challenges. Most importantly, they have received from their parents the message that the world is not a threatening place. By allowing your child to attempt to do things that are age-appropriate, you are saying, "Give it a go. There is nothing to be afraid of, so give it your best shot".

Allow your child as many opportunities as possible to explore the world, to make mistakes and to creatively find his own solutions to problems. That will ensure not only a healthy self-esteem, but a feeling of safety.

> *Paul looked sad when his dad met him after school. He told his dad that his friend Leonardo had excluded him from a game. Paul's dad immediately got furious and said he would call the school the very next day and tell the teacher to watch out for Paul and make sure it never happened again.*
>
> *Paul did not feel happy with this solution. He worried that this would make the situation worse and that Leonardo would never be his friend because Paul had "dobbed" him in. Paul had his own ideas about what he wanted to do about the situation, but felt constrained to keep them to himself.*

It would have been much more helpful for Paul's dad to have asked, "What do you want to do about it?" If Paul had said, "Nothing", his father should have accepted that and let his son work it out himself. If Paul had said, "Don't know", then his dad could have made a few suggestions like, "How about talking to

Leonardo and telling him that you want to be included?"

Paul should be left to decide for himself if he wants to take up his father's advice or not. As long as he feels supported by his father, he will find within himself the ability to work things out.

Affirmations

Hopefully, you are now ready to undo the belief that doing everything for your child is good for him. Here are some alternate slogans that you can say to yourself to assist you to see things according to a new perspective. By saying them over and over, you will soon start to perceive how to ensure your child's wellbeing in a different light which, in turn, will help you to be less protective.

Affirmation 1:
"Hard work is good for you".

By allowing my child to put in the effort required to reach his goal, I am giving him the gift of self -satisfaction. Hard work breeds many good character traits, like perseverance, diligence, persistence, and striving.

Affirmation 2:
"Self-mastery is essential for building self-esteem".

When my child completes a task, on his own, he will feel a sense of mastery over the environment. He will also feel competent and adequate in the world. These feelings will build his self-esteem and stay with him always. Even if I tell him a thousand times that he is competent, unless he experiences it through his own effort, he will not believe it.

Affirmation 3:
"Success comes through hard work".

For the majority of the world, success is a result of a lot of hard work. I will have a realistic view of success rather than buy into the myth that life can be easy, that success will fall into my child's lap.

Affirmation 4:
"Success takes time".

Humans need time to grow and develop. We do not automatically learn a skill overnight.

Affirmation 5:
"You cannot avoid the struggle".

Since sooner or later my child will be faced with a struggle that I cannot insulate him from, so it is better that he learns skills to deal with life's struggles from an early age.

Affirmation 6:
"Independence is a goal of life".

My job is to allow him to express his independent self in age-appropriate ways.

Conclusion

The best thing you can do for your child's self-esteem and to assist him to feel safe in the world is to give him skills. It is important to allow him to express his independent views and style and to work problems out for himself where appropriate. By letting go, you are providing a safety net.

By letting go appropriately, I allow my child to feel confident!

Try this:

The next time your child is grappling with a task, do not jump in to help. Instead, be interested and supportive by giving positive feedback like "You are half way there", or, "Look how much your hand writing is improving along the way", or, "This idea is uniquely yours and it shows how kind you are."

If you would like a chart of these affirmations to hang up as a daily reminder, please go to my website www.parentchildself.com and download.

Success story

Maureen walked into my consulting room in a very tense and rushed manner. She spoke rapidly and, in a few minutes, relayed the reason for her distress. She was finding her daughter Lee "impossible" in the mornings. For example, Maureen could not get her to listen and be ready for pre-school on time.

A typical morning in Maureen's home would unfold like this:

"Lee, sweetheart, it is time to brush your hair."

"O.K. but I want to have a ponytail!"

"No problem. Please come and sit down and I will brush your hair."

No sooner would Maureen begin brushing when Lee would start to whinge, "I don't want a ponytail, I want pigtails."

"Sure. Just wait one minute while I run downstairs to get a second elastic."

When she returned with two blue elastics, her

daughter would start to whine, "I don't like blue elastics, I want red ones."

"But, sweetheart, we only have one red elastic. Would you like two green ones?"

"NO! I want red!"

Back downstairs a frantic Maureen would rush to look for another red elastic. When she could not find one, she would hurry upstairs again, pleading, "Please, Lee. We have to get to school. Please wear the blue or the green. Or, if you want red, then let's do a ponytail instead, and use the elastic you want."

Maureen told me that no matter what she tried, Lee would not be appeased. Consequently, she felt like a failure.

The "old me" would have begun to think about behavioral strategies to improve the situation. The more experienced, wiser me knew that Maureen and I would need time to tease out her belief system before we could proceed.

In the first session I listened and asked exploratory questions like: "What are you trying to achieve in the morning with Lee? What would happen if you were a few minutes late for pre-school? How do you feel when you wake up in the morning to face Lee?"

Maureen's answers showed she subscribed to most of the beliefs that exhaust and stress parents.

First and foremost, she wanted to be the perfect parent, always patient, always giving and totally child-focused. She wanted Lee to feel loved and special and believed she would achieve this by buying her things, playing a game with her every day and doing things for her, such as helping her to get dressed in the morning.

In the second session, I explained my beliefs about

parenting and how it was impossible for Maureen to be perfect. Together we worked out what tools were accessible to her and what her "budget" for time, money and patience were. When Maureen understood what was realistic to aim for, she visibly relaxed. She also calmed down when it clicked in her mind that fancy elastics would not bring Lee happiness. Rather, turning the brushing hair session into quality time that they both enjoyed would be far more valuable.

The tough part was yet to come: getting Maureen to buy into the idea of being a firm captain. The entire third session was devoted to exploring what "firm" meant, what the difference between assertive and aggressive is and debunking the myth that a child is capable of making leadership decisions.

At the end of the session, I was not sure if she would come back. I was sensing disagreement and intuited that, in her heart of hearts, Maureen believed that being nice to Lee was essential even if it entailed running up and down steps to please.

With delight, and a little surprise, I watched a calm Maureen walk into my rooms for the fourth session. She confessed that she had left the previous session really confused. On the one hand, she had thought I was out of touch with modern parenting methods and that she had wasted her time and money consulting with me. On the other hand, she had felt safe with my certainty and had begun to doubt her way of seeing things, since no other method had worked thus far.

She told me, with a giggle, that the day after the session she had an epiphany. It dawned on her that I had role-modelled what a firm captain is like. I did not shout or scream or beg or back down. I had calmly stated my case and had exuded an air of authority because of my knowledge of what was right in the situation.

By copying me, she began to change her demeanor towards Lee. No more negotiation or pleading, just statements of what she expected and a limited choice. For instance, Maureen now told Lee that she had ten minutes to brush her hair. Lee could choose the style (ponytail or braid), or the color of the elastic, but not both. Once Lee picked up her mother's ability to assert herself, she no longer pushed the boundaries.

The focus became enjoying the morning time together rather than rushing, which had a calming effect on everyone. Maureen realized it did not matter at pre-school if she was a few minutes late occasionally (no-one can be punctual 100% of the time). Significantly, she encouraged Lee to take more responsibility for getting herself ready in the morning. Having her mother brush her hair became a treat that had to be "earned" by being on time.

I asked Maureen what she believed was the biggest challenge for her. She replied that it was "risking" losing Lee's love. Once she took the risk, she was surprised at how quickly Lee responded to the firmness and how much more loving their relationship had become. Maureen also said that everything I taught was common sense and easy to apply. Since she now had more realistic beliefs, she did not feel the need to run to me, or other experts, for advice. Her parenting was more relaxed and flowed organically, as she had always believed it should.

In short, *"no sweat parenting"*.

www.ingramcontent.com/pod-product-compliance
Lightning Source LLC
Chambersburg PA
CBHW060943040426
42445CB00011B/980